PLAYERS
EXPOSED

D1570555

Eugene L. Weems
Timothy R. Richardson

UNIVERSAL PUBLISHING, LLC

Published by Universal Publishing, LLC,
P.O. Box 99491, Emeryville, California 94662

A portion of the proceeds will be donated to the fight against breast cancer and victims of violent crimes.

FIRST EDITION: 2011
Cover Design: Stephani Richardson
Editor: Terri Harper, www.terristranscripts.net

ISBN: 978-0-9840456-4-8
Library of Congress Cataloguing-in-Publication Data

Universal Publishing LLC

Printed in the United States of America

TABLE OF CONTENTS

We dedicate this book to the millions of women who are searching for the way to improve their lives without the help of a man, by taking their futures into their own hands.
We hope the information shared here will help ease their way along the path of finding a good man and protecting themselves from becoming a victim of game playing men.

ACKNOWLEDGEMENTS

Annie Montgomery, Aldine Weems, Larae Weems, Henry Ridley, Sr., Henry Ridley, Jr., Madine Montgomery, Larry Bolden, James Weems, Larry Weems, Bee Johnson, Nicole Hall, Robert Swain, Timothy Blackburn, Tiana & Tiara Blackburn, and Sophia Lim. You are all dearly remembered.

I thank God for his love, patience, and for creating such a wonderful man in me. Moreover, for allowing my worldly trials and tribulations to be a learning experience and not my demise.

As always, my unconditional love is extended to my #1 girl in the world, my aunty **Mrs. Betty Sue Ridley.** Tee-Tee, love don't have nothing to do with that two-hundred seventy-six thousand dollars. I'm gonna need that back.

My love and respect go out to the following people: Michael Payton, Kisha Gray, Antralisa Shavette Alexander, Thelma Adams, Elizabeth Hall, Andrea Calloway, Alicia *Black Diamond* Griffin, Gwendolyn James, KeyonJane Whittle, Janet A. Berger, Nate J.B. Brown, Marquichea Burns, Theodore *Ted* Cole, Sheila Devereaux, Chi Ali Griffith, Heather Hall, Demond Hammond, Boobie Jacobs, Michael & Yolanda Jacobs, Ray Jacobs, Demetrius McClendon, Corey *C-Murder* Miller, Lamond Moore, Sean *Frisco* Moran, Threathere Pickett, Terry *T.P.* Prince, Debbie Ridley, Steven Ridley, Stephani Richardson, Timothy *TipToe* Richardson, Curtis Schuler, Ambre Shaw-Sanders, Crystal Shaw, Izana Shaw, Shamar Shaw, Sharel Shaw, Messiah Sims, Delbert Smith, Charles *C.W.* Webb, Demarko Weems-Hall, Ebony L. Weems-Mickel, Kishana Weems, Leonard Weems, Sheryl Rene Weems, Nakesha Whittle.

Eugene L. Weems

ACKNOWLEDGEMENTS

First and before anything, I thank my creator and Lord God, for planting within me the insight and strength to change.

Thank Universal Publishing LLC for providing my co-author and I the podium by which the truth will be heard.

Mostly, I thank my wife and children for not judging me or turning their love away from me in my times of poor choices.

As well, I praise their strength in the face of my embarrassments and shame to our family name with my participation in the opposites of justice and righteousness.

I've found the right direction to go in order to clean up the mess I've made. Though it's a long journey back, I promise to fix everything I've ruined. Bear with me.

I wish to thank my mother for all she has done to encourage me to stand up and be accounted for. I thank my father for giving me the confidence of royalty and teaching me to be a leader. *Always take the wheel and drive yourself, or don't complain when someone else is driving your life to the dumps.*

You're right, Dad. I will always be a trailblazer; a leader!

And to another great thinker and savvy businessman whom I respect greatly, my friend, my co-author, and my brother from a different mother, Mr. Eugene Weems. Your efforts and ideals have created a pivotal moment in my life, and without you, none of this could have happened. Thank you, Bruh!!

And in closing, I thank my children and the mothers who share them with me; thank my entire family for unconditionally loving me; especially thank my supporters, readers, and fans for understanding me, even though I'm so different of an author than most. To you all, please accept my very special thanks.

T. Rich
Timothy R. Richardson

WARNING!!

Before you begin gazing your eyes on the following pages of this book, please be aware that this is not just your ordinary book on the subject of how men manipulate women and how to recognize and avoid being a victim.

This is a book that depicts this game of the lifestyle of being a player in its raw form, with straightforward descriptions of how the game is played.

You may find the content to be disturbing, disrespectful, degrading, shocking, and a little overwhelming. In these pages you will not find inspirational stories and spiritual verse. What you will find are the answers to the questions women have about men who are skilled at the game.

This book will give you the insight that your mind and body may need to help you avoid being vulnerable, due to the fact that you are naive.

Know who you're dealing with. See through the game play. Here you will learn how to recognize it when you see it. Now you will see it before it happens.

Be informed!!

INTRODUCTION

We, the authors, begin this book by saying, Hello there, Beautiful.

We express that in all honesty. We understand you may be wondering, how would they know if I am beautiful or not, when it's visually impossible to know who's reading this string of printed words, let alone being able to determine your beauty.

We, the authors, witnessed many of the most divine wonders of this world, from the biggest mountains to the deepest valleys. We believe in a power greater than ourselves created the most beautiful things on this earth, from the smallest flower to the greatest thunderstorm, and you.

We can appreciate everything fascinating as much as we can everything horrific. We strongly believe women are the most wonderful and beautiful creations of all. We think of all women on the face of the earth as beautiful. So, if you are a woman reading this, such adoration is merited.

We feel that no day should pass without a man expressing his appreciation for your existence; showing his love, respect and admiration for such delicate, beautiful, intelligent, fascinating individuals who are able to produce life and to nurture the world with their love.

Most of all things created, frightening and pleasurable alike, are all deserving of the admiration and respect, due appropriate applause, pause and attention.

In this new millennium, too many men have adopted an adolescent state of mind of being players, pimps, macks, playboys and gigolos.

This only leads to an unhealthy, manipulative, and hurtful relationship for the women who may be encompassed by the intentional manipulation of men with the sole intent of some form of profitable gain.

Many men of today's society have forfeited their ethics, moral principles, and respect for our underappreciated feminine counterparts: Beautiful Women.

This book was composed exclusively for women, to help educate them so they can recognize, identify, and avoid being victimized by the womanizing, game running players. This one of a kind "Tell All" book will introduce the reader into a world of finesse, nonchalance, and long con manipulation perfected to a natural way of life, luxury, wealth and more.

This book will present to you subliminal questions and definite reasonable doubt that would not breed insecurities, but surely incite skepticism.

Exercising your right to be informed does not make you an untrusting and paranoid individual; it makes you an informed and cautious person.

Some of the methods described in this book are driven by naive and trusting women. Some are merely bluffs, like the finger in the pocket phony pistol. Others play on the deepest level of what most women desire; an honest, trusting, loyal, loving relationship with a man who can be a friend, a lover, moral and emotional supporter, through the good times and the bad.

The information that you are about to be introduced to may strike you as disturbing, shocking, repulsive and degrading. The absolute truth in its raw form had to be told.

Who can tell it better than those who have implemented the powers of persuasion and earned a living from manipulating women for their own profitable gain?

Who could better teach you how to avoid falling prey to a womanizer, than someone who has perfected the art himself?

The question is, can you handle the truth?

Can you be honest enough with yourself to admit that you are or have been a victim of the game?

Self-honesty is the first step to freeing your mind of denial and moving toward change.

WHEN THE AUTHOR
TIMOTHY R. RICHARDSON
SPEAKS

Eugene L. Weems, Timothy R. Richardson

WHEN THE AUTHOR TIMOTHY R. RICHARDSON SPEAKS

What you are about to read is the raw, uncut real about me, Mr. Timothy "TipToe" Richardson. The following will *not* be simplified for your easy reading pleasure. I will speak bluntly and very matter-of-factly. This is not a "For Dummies Manual." This is my life being shared among the masses for purposes of savin' a few. Why? Because of how much I've done to upset the equilibrium of the world's energy in my circle, and being a believer in Karma (Yin & Yang), I felt a need to create balance on my behalf. Why? Because now I have daughters that I fear so much for in being a victim to a greedy, slicker-than-grease-and-baby-oil, master manipulator like I used to be. So yeah, this is me trying to wash away some of the dirt I've done and making things as right as I can. So recognize my therapy and use me for your own personal gain, and let's see what went around, come back around in a positive reincarnation.

I grew up to the age of four in the household of a pimp, my father. Surrounded by domestic violence; witnessing the abuse of women and living in a luxury that as a child I grew up to glorify. My father assaulted my mother to a point that she felt was unforgivable and she decided to put so much distance between herself and my father that we ended up moving from Fresno, California, to Oakland.

Now, understand, Oakland has always been known as the land of the pimp, players, hustlers, ballaz, shot callers and bank robbers.

So go figure. A young, wide-eyed son of a pimp running wild on a single mother, picking up bad habits like metal to a magnet. *Soaking up game* like a sponge, and keepin' my boots laced to the latest come-up.

Not quite finding my groove by the age of nine, still searching for the Game God to bless me with my direction, I turned to selling drugs and totin' thumpaz. I quickly found myself serving time in juvenile facilities for drugs and firearm possession. Then, one day I was arrested for shooting up a house and charged with several serious felonies, publicly displayed on the nightly news channels as being an under-age suspect involved in a highly publicized crime dubbed *Nightmare on Birch Street.* (I did most of my crime in my neighborhood on 96th Avenue and Birch Street.)

For my part in *Nightmare on Birch Street,* I was sent away to serve time in 1986. I returned to living life as I knew it to be normal in 1993. During my incarceration through a state facility for felonious youth (California Youth Authority), I adopted new learned behaviors that, again, I accepted as a normal way of life. Fighting to survive and avoid being a victim of in-custody rapes or molestations from older inmates, or being a victim of robbery of my personal possessions and other forms of bullying by bigger and stronger inmates was a daily practice.

I suppose in my spare time alone, when I read books and enjoyed magazines filled with half-naked women, is where I began to manifest this *ism* that I must've been born with. Looking at what America's image of beauty is inside of magazines and on television had sparked a hunger within me that could only be satiated once I was released. That image of beauty defined by our American media was of white women. Blond hair, blue eyes, petite physique, Caucasian women were the stereotypical model of what a man of prominence and power would have as a lover. They are the models, escorts, sexy centerfolds and naughty nurses in almost every TV

4

show, magazine and sex-filled romance novel. The writing was on the wall. When I get out, I'm getting me a white girl. And I did. And just like most young teens, she and I had thoughts of just being alone. Running away and living on our own. Now, how would we get the money to do so? Well, I was familiar with the drug dealing life, remember?

So, in came drug dealing; buying drugs from low-level dealers at almost wholesale prices to sell at almost below retail prices to make fast money. Since I was the one with the criminal record and feared being re-arrested, in comes the trusting young white girl, ready to do her part to get us financially stable enough to run away. So while she would sell the drugs with me as security half a block away, most of the users that had come to buy drugs would also offer her money to come along with them for sex as well. Of course, her answer was always, *No, I have a boyfriend."* And I, wanting this young beautiful American goddess (white girl) to myself, would take offense to anyone wanting my girlfriend and protect her with acts of violence or fits of rage against those dope users.

Eventually, the drug trade began to slow, and she and I, living above our means in hotels, eating out in restaurants two and three times daily, began to get expensive. This financial strain began to cause dissention and distance between us, and for the most part, between my feelings for her. So alternate earnings choices were considered.

In my mind, seeing many players, macks and pimps riding in nice luxury cars filled to capacity with women that were under the pimp's strict command and rules. I began with my persuasion of why my young white girlfriend and I should enter into the sex trade. So I conned her with a bunch of, *If you love me, you'll do this,* and, *We could only do this hustle for a little while, save up some money and move away.* And before we knew it, I was a pimp and she was my very first hoe (prostitute).

5

From that day forward, I learned every rule and tactic used in the Pimp Game to get ahead. I learned every single power of persuasion that I could use in my favor to manipulate women to my advantage. Even the women I had no intention of introducing to the prostitution game, I found a way to convince them to give me a minimum of $2,000 weekly. Most of the women that decided full well and on their own to furnish me with lavish gifts and money did so merely just to be in my presence. Why? Because my charm was borderline fairytale romance to these women of my capture.

My introduction was not that of a pimp. It was that of a hopeless romantic. I would send invitations for lunch along with round trip plane tickets to neighboring states. We would fly out after a breakfast in our home state, arrive at our destination and have lunch in a steak house and then tour the city's fashion district for shopping. Then, as evening fell, take a limo to a neighboring city to enjoy a casual dinner experience with fine libations. Then, head back to the airport for a return flight home. The fairytale date would end with me, as a gentleman, walking her to her front door and asking only for a goodnight kiss. A day or two later, invite her to perhaps an inner city festival, dinner and four- or five-star hotel reservation to enjoy dancing and room service, bubble bathing, massage and mind-blowing sex.

I would return her home like the gentleman of days prior, and allow days to pass without a call or a visit. Why? Because I needed to build a longing in my absence. I wanted her to want me, miss me, and wonder is it something she did wrong? Was it the sex? Was she not skilled or pleasing enough? When I finally contacted her, my reasoning would simply be the fact that I was busy working to maintain my financial stability, and also that I was afraid she could no longer respect, enjoy or appreciate me if she knew what I did for a living.

6

And after being such a gentleman or a dream come true for her in the figure of a man, I'd wait for her to say, *It doesn't matter what you do.* She would say this because in her wildest imagination she could never think I was into something horrendous, illegal, or degrading; because, after all, I'm such a sweetheart and Prince Charming.

So, she declares that she wants to spend more time with me. That's when I downplay what I do. What a pimp is. Pimp is such a nasty word to people sometimes, so I use a nonchalant approach. I say something like, *Well, I'm sort of an escort promoter. I'm something to the tone of an adult relations guru, if you will.* And if she's an intelligent, mature, middle to upper class woman, I sometimes just play it straight. I just tell it like it is and claim it. *Baby, I'm a real live pimp!*

Now, one or two things can happen when she's faced with the real truth. One, she can pretend she thinks I'm joking and leave me room to clean it up with lies and deny it so that she feels better about herself for wanting to continue seeing me; in her mind thinking that she could help or change me. Or, two, she can admit that she's never known a real pimp before and pretend to be fascinated by this, claiming or asking that I would never pimp her. Whatever choice she makes other than refusing to associate with me any longer is an indication that she is infatuated or fascinated by the idea of having her very own Bad Boy.

That's when my games begin. This is when I begin to tell her things like, *I've never been with a bitch that didn't pay me.* Or, if I wanted to be polite and lose the ghetto language and use a little class and finesse, I might say something like, *I've never been in a relationship before, or even spent a lot of time with a woman that could not offer me as much as I could offer her. I'm old fashioned, but not ancient.*

I believe a woman should be honest, cherish, and *obey* her man, but I also believe a woman should let the man manage the finances, call the shots, and approve any and all spending. The man in most cultures is the one who receives the dowry for accepting the woman as his partner, not the other way around. If her credit is good and she wants to claim me as her man, then I should be able to represent her to the best of my ability.

Big Daddy needs a new car, truck or motorcycle, off the lot! She should worry about the payments. Give it to me as a gift. Why? For the same reasons the love sick, soft ass, sprung chicken, square ass businessman gives the $15,000 tennis bracelet or the big ass engagement ring to the female; to show his love, respect, and to please her. Should a female be treated any different in this day and age of equal opportunism? Shit! I'm slanging the best sex a woman could ever imagine, with moves I've perfected to a science. Remember, I've made a million dollar business out of the sex trade. I know what a woman wants and needs. It's worth the four grand she showers me with. Her money can't give to her these uncontrollable orgasms and seize control of her heart, mind, body and soul. But I can.

Can you put a price on love or happiness? Exactly. There was a time when I could. I leased it at a minimum of $2,000 a week. I didn't care how they got the money. Wouldn't bother me if they had to steal, beg, borrow, or even take shit to the pawn shops. I only wanted mine. Ya see, I always felt as though every woman in the world wondered at least once if she was pretty enough to be admired as a model. Every woman wants at least once to feel as though she is beautiful enough to be paid based on her looks alone. Be it through being chosen to show on a commercial, magazine, or movie. Or even if she might be pretty enough for at least one man in this world to want to give or buy her everything her heart desired.

So, yeah, I was the guy to make you feel that way. I didn't care if she had an elephant trunk growin' out the center of her forehead. I would never make her feel anything short of a super model. Who would want to walk away from a man that praises you like so? I would put a wig on a pig, a gorilla in garters, and sell snake hips and turkey lips to a vegetarian. I could talk a hamburger out of his buns for fun. *Slick lip with a golden tongue* is how I was born. Why not utilize my talents?

Well, that's what I thought it was. So, being a kid from the bottom barrel of the ghetto, the son of a pimp and a single mother caught in the struggle, I saw no wrong in going strong with creative ways to provide for myself. So what if I had to use sex as the podium by which I preached the good words of pimpin' and persuading my prey to obey and pay. You'd be surprised what a woman would agree to surrender to while under the influence of good dick. They say love is blind, but good sex is hypnotizing. I could leave a woman more addicted than your rawest form of heroin; and while she's screaming out in ecstasy and agony, pleasure and pain, yelling her ooohs and aahhs, I would ask her questions and proposition her to aid me in getting rich, and for her to agree to do anything in the world I asked of her, and while my in-and-out-and-all-about plunges deeply, it was nothing for her to throw in a few *Yes, Daddys* and *I promises*.

After sex, I would ask her if she meant everything she said. Well, not completely knowing what she signed up for, I then would encourage her to trust me, ask her if she could see herself loving me enough to live and die for me. Who would say no? Thinking rationally, any woman would assume I'm speaking hypothetically and just roll with it. She would say yes. That's when I would declare that I'm not even asking that much of her; that I would never ask her nor put her in a position to be the victim of any sort of harm or danger for me. After all, I only want her to live for me.

9

I would then go into my song and dance about how overrated sex is. How, if I based my love, respect, or admiration for her on sex, that it automatically sets an expiration date, because if sex is my reason, then when the pussy dries up, gets old, or is no longer as good as it used to be, then the love is over.

So my love would be based on her willingness to invest in a future filled with happily ever afters; that we should fill our life together with memories of travels, luxury living, extravagant spending and enjoying all the wonders of the world, because life is so short. So we should grab life in a headlock and do with it whatever we wish.

Nobody wants to be born, live, and die without seeing all that was created on a planet for our marvel, enjoyment, and pleasure. If I spent 30 years trying to be rich the hard way, added to the 20-plus years I had been, then more than half my life would be gone before I actually begin to enjoy living it. Who grows to be 100 years old these days? So living today like it's my last is always my first choice. And you?

So, once she agrees to see my methods, I invite her into a world of internet, late nights, private shows, casinos, islands, and money by the stacks coming in hand over fist. All this data coming in so fast, it's hard to process. So before she could talk herself out of it, in comes the second round of mind blowing sex. Keepin' her *pipe drunk* is my intention. Little does she know, soon she'll be payin' upwards of $1,000 daily to be with me, hoping that on a particular day, around once a month, I might *service her.*

Once she's officially *turned out,* then comes the teaching of the rules.

Staying in pocket is rule number one. Never should a woman of mine make eye contact with another man who's not a paying customer. Never should she speak with any man unless her sole intention is to walk away from him with some of his money, or gifts with the receipts for possible return, to make her daily pay quota.

Never should she do any *hoe socializing* (socializing with other prostitutes) unless her intention is to persuade the woman she's talking to into choosing to join my stable.

Those are to name a few. The rules are so many that this book could end up as long as the Old and New Testament, so we won't go there. My only intention of this insight on myself was to enlighten you of my credibility to advise or educate on these subjects ahead. Sort of, what I would call displaying my degrees in Pimpology and powerful persuasion and manipulation.

So, exercise your right to be informed, protected, and prepared for any and all trickeration, manipulation, and slick talkin' players.

The following is the gospel truth in Players Exposed!! And the methods used to manipulate women...

Mr. Timothy "TipToe" Richardson

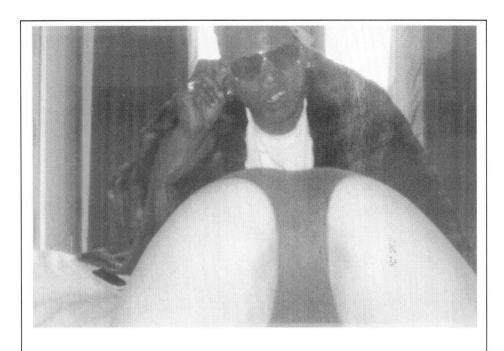

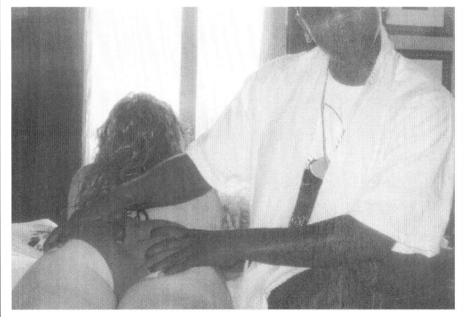

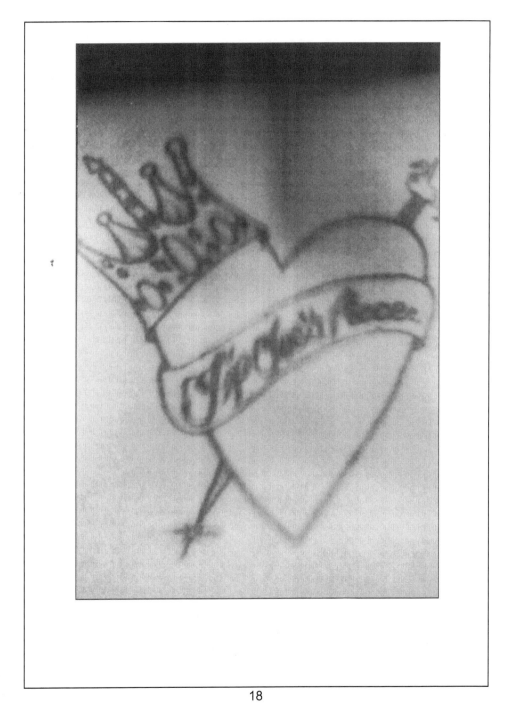

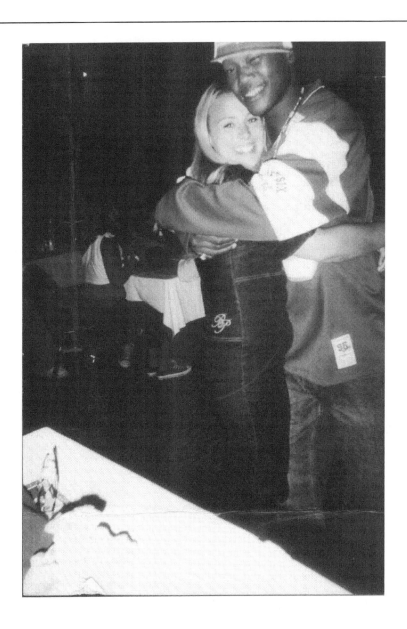

21

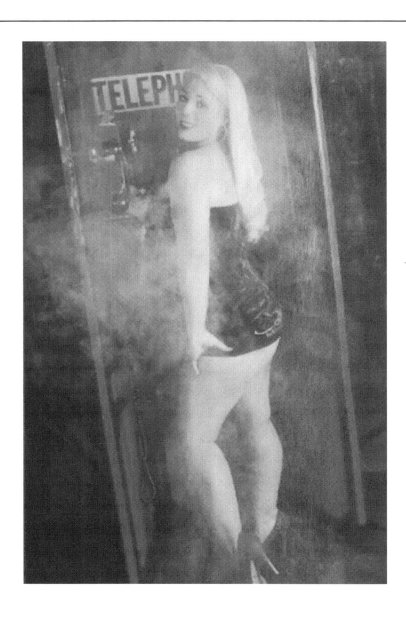

Eugene L. Weems, Timothy R. Richardson

SUPERIOR COURT OF CALIFORN \
COUNTY OF SANTA CLARA \
SAN JOSE FACILITY \
COMPLAINT FOR ARREST WARRANT(S) \
TIMOTHY RAYMOND RICHARDSON DZAƏ14 ⅋ \
ROBERT FORREST HENDRICKS DPM972

THE PEOPLE OF THE STATE OF CALIFORNIA,

Plaintiff,

vs.

TIMOTHY RAYMOND RICHARDSON (7/21/1974), \
331 S. JEFFERSON STREET #6, DIXON, CA 95620 \
ROBERT FORREST HENDRICKS (9/8/1980), \
3126 HOOD STREET, OAKLAND, CA 94605

Defendant(s)

CC930225

FELONY COMPLAINT

ENDORSED FILED

DA NO: 090100009 \
CEN

JAN 0 2 2009

DAVID H. YAMASAKI \
Chief Executive Officer/Clerk \
Superior Court of CA County of Santa Clara

TR WARR \
RH WARR — A. MENDOZA DEPUTY

PROTECTIVE ORDER

The undersigned is informed and believes that:

COUNT 1

On or about and between November 29, 2008 and December 18, 2008, in the County of Santa Clara, State of California, the crime of HUMAN TRAFFICKING, in violation of PENAL CODE SECTION 236.1(a), a Felony, was committed by TIMOTHY RAYMOND RICHARDSON AND ROBERT FORREST HENDRICKS who did unlawfully deprive and violate the personal liberty of another person, namely, Jane Doe I, with the intent to effect and maintain a felony violation of Penal Code section 266h and to obtain forced labor and services of the victim.

COUNT 2

On or about and between November 29, 2008 and December 18, 2008, in the County of Santa Clara, State of California, the crime of HUMAN TRAFFICKING, in violation of PENAL CODE SECTION 236.1(a), a Felony, was committed by TIMOTHY RAYMOND RICHARDSON AND ROBERT FORREST HENDRICKS who did unlawfully deprive and violate the personal liberty of another person, namely, Jane Doe II, with the intent to effect and maintain a felony violation of Penal Code section 266h and to obtain forced labor and services of the victim.

Page 1

COUNT 3

On or about and between November 29, 2008 and December 18, 2008, in the County of Santa Clara, State of California, the crime of PIMPING WHERE THE PROSTITUTE IS AN ADULT, in violation of PENAL CODE SECTION 266h(a), a Felony, was committed by TIMOTHY RAYMOND RICHARDSON AND ROBERT FORREST HENDRICKS who did, knowing Jane Doe I to be a prostitute, live and derive support and maintenance from the earnings and proceeds of the prostitution and from money loaned and advanced to and charged against the person by a keeper, manager and inmate of a house and other place where prostitution was practiced and allowed, and solicited and received compensation for soliciting for the prostitute.

It is further alleged that the defendant(s) is/are not eligible for probation and suspension of sentence within the meaning of Penal Code section 1203.065(a).

COUNT 4

On or about and between November 29, 2008 and December 18, 2008, in the County of Santa Clara, State of California, the crime of PIMPING WHERE THE PROSTITUTE IS AN ADULT, in violation of PENAL CODE SECTION 266h(a), a Felony, was committed by TIMOTHY RAYMOND RICHARDSON AND ROBERT FORREST HENDRICKS who did, knowing Jane Doe II to be a prostitute, live and derive support and maintenance from the earnings and proceeds of the prostitution and from money loaned and advanced to and charged against the person by a keeper, manager and inmate of a house and other place where prostitution was practiced and allowed, and solicited and received compensation for soliciting for the prostitute.

It is further alleged that the defendant(s) is/are not eligible for probation and suspension of sentence within the meaning of Penal Code section 1203.065(a).

Any defendant, including a juvenile, who is convicted of and pleads guilty and no contest to any felony offense, including any attempt to commit the offense, charged in this complaint or information is required to provide buccal swab samples, right thumbprints and a full palm print impression of each hand, and any blood specimens or other biological samples required pursuant to the DNA and Forensic Identification Database and Data Bank Act of 1998 and Penal Code section 296, et seq.

Further, attached and incorporated by reference are official reports and documents of a law enforcement agency which the complainant believes establish probable cause for the arrest of defendant TIMOTHY RAYMOND RICHARDSON, for the above-listed crimes. Wherefore, A WARRANT OF ARREST IS REQUESTED.

Further, attached and incorporated by reference are official reports and documents of a law enforcement agency which the complainant believes establish probable cause for the arrest of defendant ROBERT FORREST HENDRICKS, for the above-listed crimes. Wherefore, A WARRANT OF ARREST IS REQUESTED.

Complainant therefore requests that the defendant(s) be dealt with according to law.

I certify under penalty of perjury that the above is true and correct.

Executed on January 2, 2009, in SANTA CLARA County, California.

Warrant received for service by:

on _____

Cash or Bond $_____

Clarke C4489
(Clarke C4489)
SCPD (408) 615-4800 0813425
ALVARADO/ D432/ FELONY/ lm

_____
JUDGE OF THE SUPERIOR COURT

Eugene L. Weems, Timothy R. Richardson

SLIDIN' THROUGH THE BLADE

Eugene L. Weems, Timothy R. Richardson

SLIDIN' THROUGH THE BLADE

This is where you either choose to ride with pimpin, or, if you're scared or unprepared to cruise the back alleys and boulevards of pimpin' and hoeing, then this is where you put the book down and back away from my ride.

If you're still holding your ticket for a ride on a pimp side, then shut up, get in, and don't be acting like no square. You ready? Shut the door, then. Let's ride.

What's yo' name, anyways? For the record, I am *TipToe "Da Truth"* in the street game, but *Big D.D. "The Law"* is my pimp handle. What I'm about to do is take you through the very avenues of where pimps are up and hoes are down, so you can experience a day in the life on *The Track*. Picture this:

You just opened the door of a brand spankin' new Cadillac Escalade SUV. The latest R&B soul hit is thumping semi-loudly through six twelve-inch woofers and four six-by-nines. Windows are up, air conditioning keepin' us chill in the summer's heat. That new car smell is adding to our comfort, and the whole city surrounding us is playing on the big screen windows of Big Daddy's Caddy. By the way, the pimp handle *Big D.D. "The Law"* stood for *Big Dick Daddy "The Law"* and was dubbed because there weren't many pimps in the game still living by the original 32 Bars of Pimping. Therefore, I was familiar with the methods of placing a hoe under *pimp arrest* and convincing her current pimp or management to comply and release her to my custody.

31

Now, me personally, well, I took the game very seriously, so I respected and therefore enforced the rules to the letter. Hence known as *The Law*.

Okay, now you have to lean your seat back some, try to align your head with the doorjamb that divides the passenger door with the rear passenger door, because we are in Oakland now. Sitting duck with your head a big ass target in the window could get you shot in the face, so please don't be such a square. Lean back and protect your crown. It's okay to peep over the windowsill and check out the possible, but this ain't no petting zoo, so don't paste your face on the window. These hoes see a pimp on the move, they gonna scatter like roaches when the lights come on. Just shine for 'em, baby, and watch them choose. I'm about to give them a reason to see how life is better with me. Turn that music down for me and watch this, as I roll my window down and mack at a lazy bitch sittin' on her ass.

"Aye! Wuzzup, lil' darling? Why you sittin' on it like you don't want it? I know you hear me. That's fine, you can ignore pimpin' if you wish, and I can respect you're trying to maintain pocket. Cool. I'm just curious to why you're half-assin'. You're trying to follow the rules and not holla back at a pimp; good job, I commend you. All the same, though, you're sittin' on your ass and ain't tryin' to make no money, be seen or advertise, which means either you ain't happy with your daddy or you're bred for the bed and not for the track. Let me keep you in a five star hotel making *racks* (thousands) on your back. I can prep you an exit plan for this game where you never look back. You just can't be happy where you at, so let me pick you up and dust you off, put some shine on you and hold you up for the whole world to see. I can make you a celebrity overnight. You won't get another chance to walk away from your old life and into the new, so don't sit there and do nothing when you can change your situation right now. You're too beautiful to just sit out here in the neighborhood jumpin' in and out of cars for fifties. You can leave with me right now and in two weeks in a five star suite, you'll be a powerhouse with men groveling at your feet. I bet you ain't never made twenty grand in just over a week. I won't keep giving you action at fuckin' with a real one. It's your turn to make a change for yourself, lil' mama."

That's when I shout my cell phone number out once or twice while she acts as if she's ignoring me. But chances are she will never forget my number in case her current pimp pisses her off. Yeah, yeah, I know it's a shitty way for a man to treat women. I used to tell myself that this isn't the hustle for me, but the game don't wait. So, if it isn't me giving her an opportunity to allow me to manage her, then it's another hustler making thousands, and me standing in the free food line at the local church food bank.

Give a starving third world child a chance to snatch a big meal by breakin' the law, and maybe even getting his right hand chopped off, or standing in a line of 300 to 400 people waiting on a small cup of rice, and see what their choice would be. Next time you see him, everything he does will be with his left hand.

Sure, I know I'm not a starving third world country kid, but I sure as hell ain't tryin' to wait around like one in our great American country, either. So, it is what it is. Well, at least at that time that's how I was thinking.

Poor girls...shit; poor me!!

I say that because I was a monster in a world that was so normal to me that my reality became that of many of the women who needed help, not another selfish so-called *manager*. As you walk deeper into this world I am guiding you through, I will completely understand and agree with your disgust of me and who I was. Please try to remember, though, that I am no longer that individual. The only way I feel I could ever make amends for the destruction I've caused is to begin making repairs by warning those caught in this cycle how to avoid the traps.

The sole intention of this book is to allow readers exclusive access to a world they otherwise would never be permitted to see, in an effort to expose the lures and manipulation that trap those unsuspecting women. I dig deep into the realism of the lifestyle, language, and attitude in an effort to allow you (the reader) an opportunity to personally feel the experience from the inside of this underworld activity.

What you just experienced was some of the simple work of a pimp saying as much as he could to any hoe working the blade that would listen, hoping that perhaps one thing he said in his nonstop rambling would affect the thinking of at least one working girl to call his number. If, by chance, one does, then his probability of *knockin' her* just improved by eighty percent. So his next step would be *The Knock...*

The Knock is when he has officially convinced her to submit to his rule, to work for him, to obey his every command. This is just another one to add to his stable of earners. Once she has joined his entourage of working girls, he is off to *slide through the blade* elsewhere, to meet and greet another hoe in the street.

It's a thankless job, but a community service all the same. I wonder how many horny, mentally unstable men I may have prevented from raping or kidnapping innocent, unsuspecting women by providing an outlet for him with a woman who could cure him in one simple exchange for payment (I used to ask myself, in an effort to justify this atrocious behavior).

WHEN THE AUTHOR
EUGENE L. WEEMS
SPEAKS

Eugene L. Weems, Timothy R. Richardson

WHEN THE AUTHOR EUGENE L. WEEMS
SPEAKS

Although I come from a lineage of educated, career oriented, respectful, hard-working, supportive, Christian rooted, loving family, who made every attempt to shield me from the unconventional lifestyles of the world, their attempt was practically impossible, being that I was born and raised in Las Vegas, Nevada, a city well-known for being a single man's paradise and a married man's sure way to divorce court, and the place where dreams no longer had to be fantasy.

I had relatives who were considered outcasts, bad breeds, black sheep and disappointments to our distinctive family good characteristics and reputation. They were gangsters, players, drug dealers and pimps, who would faithfully introduce and attempt to fill my mind with negative encouragements to their way of living.

Just like any young man growing up, I took heed to the fascination of their lifestyle and soaked every trick of the trade up like a sponge and stored it somewhere in my mind for later use, if need be. There was no doubt Vegas was the place to make a mint of that American green quickly and cash in on a fast retirement plan without a corporate 401K. But that was only if you could avoid falling prey to the many deceptions that lay in the silent shadows next to the broad opportunities for success.

My life had begun to take a dramatic twist after the death of my grandmother, the woman who I adored and loved with the depth of my soul. The woman who raised me after my mother passed away when I was five years old. She was the foundation that kept me grounded.

I had ventured into the street life, which had introduced me to the life of crime and incarceration. Getting back on my square was somewhat impossible. I had been too deep in the game on every level in the world of organized crime to attempt to step away. I was now a player in every sense of the word, but found pleasures in making love to women. A true gigolo I had become in the realm of my reality. My only objective had been to finesse the panties off my succulent prey and seduce them for my own sexual cravings, but my intimate caresses and deep invading of the soul that evoked so many sexual sensations of pleasure to a passion that claimed the mind and body of my victims had been lucrative.

Most of my victims that I once lustfully desired, cunningly made indirect propositions with expensive jewelry, clothes and financial gifts to lure me into spending more quality time with them, which always consisted of heavy breathing, cries of pleasurable pain and two nude bodies being drenched in the intimacy of gratification. I reassured myself this was the life where I could never become bored. There was never a dull moment. Tedious, yes, because the excitement and gifts never ended and my many options of pleasure with women were physically and mentally exhausting.

What really captivated my mind and sealed my fate to such a lifestyle was the very moment a snow bunny *chose up* on me with a mink coat, a black Escalade SUV, and $9,000 of that pure unadulterated American cash. I remember it as if it was just yesterday, removing the wad from her underwear drawer and shuffling through the new style big-face Franklins just to admire their substance and authority. It was New Year's Eve and one of my lady friends hit me on the hip with the desire to bring in the new year with me. Before I could reject her invitation, she informed me that she had a gift for me. She knew just how much I love receiving gifts, especially ones from her. She made it worth my while. Every time. I was excited and curious to see how she was going to top the ten grand she laced my pockets with three weeks ago, so I gave her the green light to come on through.

She did just that, making an unannounced entrance into my home. She smiled up at me with lustful eyes when I noticed her and an unknown female standing in my living room. She gently took me in her arms, pressing her body up against mine, and whispered in my ear, "There is your gift right there." She gestured toward her friend. This time I took a much longer gaze at my gift. The attractive snow bunny who had a banging body that went along with a gorgeous face. The black leather pants suit she wore showed more than her gifted curves. I couldn't help but stare below her navel at what looked like a camel's foot pressing against the soft leather that hugged her body. She noticed my approval, but said nothing as she offered me a smile.

I felt my nature rising, picturing her naked body connecting together with mine. I wondered how her cries of intensity sounded in the heat of some exotic thug loving, and what level of freak she was in the bedroom. It was obvious she couldn't keep her eyes off the huge bulge that formed in my pants. I motioned for her to spin around so I could view her full figure.

"Daddy, you like what you see?" She had such a sweet voice, not giving me the opportunity to respond before inviting herself into my arms and robbing my lips for some sweetness. I didn't reject her kiss or the body I now held tightly, but pressed my hardness up against her stomach. I looked deep into her eyes and began running sweet game. I knew it was cookies when she reached into her cleavage and took out a small stack of folded bills and asked me to hold it for her. That New Year's Eve ended with many wonderful and unforgettable experiences and the new year was brought in with a bang.

It was now official. I was a connoisseur of every level of the game, and there was no turning back. The inducement of a woman's pleasure and reward was hardwired into my psyche.

41

Eugene L. Weems, Timothy R. Richardson

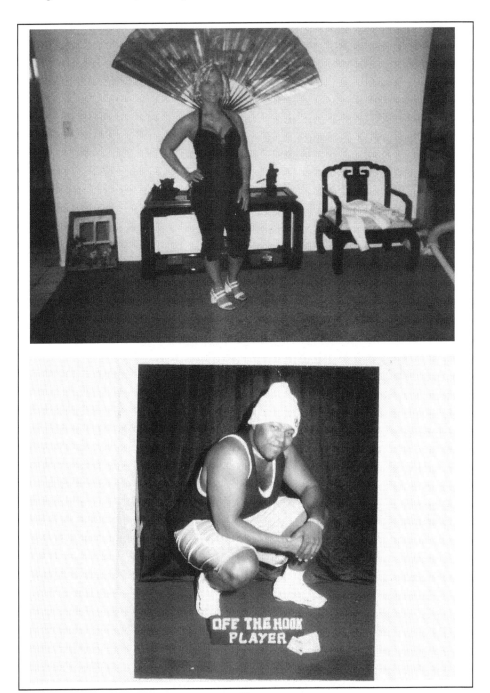

LICKIN' A HONEY DIP

Eugene L. Weems, Timothy R. Richardson

LICKIN' A HONEY DIP

Lickin' a honey dip is slanguage for *breakin' a professional square bear.* This is when I meet and get closely acquainted with a mature, professional career woman who is well-to-do financially and independently. I would charm and preferably get intimately familiar with her.

After spending time with her and *investing* my own time and even my own money on dates and small shopping ventures to get her comfortable with the ideal of seeing no hesitation in my willingness to share or show my financial freedom.

I would also begin to surprise her with gifts I had purchased at malls or while away on trips out of town. When I gave them to her, I would say things like, *I was thinking of you when I saw this and thought you might look nice in it*, or, *Babe, you deserve the finest of everything, and this may have easily been the finest gift that city had to offer, so I wanted it to belong to you.* These comments, as corny as they may seem, are only seeds to plant that I would harvest from in the near future. Soon would come the day when I would recoup my small investments, and more.

I would perhaps take her for lunch and then *just so happen* to drive by a car or motorcycle dealership. I'd make it seem like a spontaneous pleasure to stop in and take a look. That's when I would act like a kid in a candy store, hoping she would enjoy seeing me so happy that she encourages me to make a purchase. I would share imaginative tales of how much fun I would like to have with her on either this new motorcycle or in this new convertible, trying to excite her. Then I would make tons of excuses as to why I, myself, couldn't make the purchase due to current financial investments or credit

49

hassles I'm trying to resolve. If she still doesn't volunteer to use her credit or do this as a gift to me now, I would reinforce the idea of how nice it would've been as we are leaving.

That's when I would appear to lose interest in the happy attitude I displayed just minutes ago. Lose interest in our date and just basically display a sort of detachment, period. This act would continue until she mentions the car or motorcycle issue. My distance would continue into nonchalance and vague answers until she volunteers to make the purchase for me. If she doesn't, I would come up with a reason why I must cancel our date and begin talking about what I wish I could do with my current predicament to acquire my desire.

My sole intention is to lay a guilt trip on her so thick that she would do almost anything to see me happy as I was at the dealership. Long story short, she would eventually give in. Why wouldn't she? I've bought gifts for her. I make her feel young again. For all she knows, I am financially secure, and I am so much fun to be with.

So, yes, I end up getting what I want. Almost the same methods can be used in getting women to do anything you want after you get her enthralled in your personality, addicted to your character, and especially dependent on your sexual abilities. Like for instance, investing in your business ideals or giving large sums of money for whatever your needs are. Bottom line: when it comes to the art of *lickin' a honey dip,* you better be sure that your target has honey to dip into and lick.

Don't waste your time if she ain't got a dime!

KNOCKIN' 'EM OFF LINE

Eugene L. Weems, Timothy R. Richardson

KNOCKIN' 'EM OFF LINE

Being in the streets or walking through public attractions is not the only way for a player to find a playing field.

Let's just take for instance: a prisoner. A guy who is completely isolated from society. Unless he personally knows someone he can send snail mail to at their home or P.O. Box address, then his ability to meet new women is extremely challenging, to say the least. Wouldn't you think?

I thought so, too, until I became a prisoner. Being the magnificent orator that I am, combined with my entrepreneurial ingenuity, I knew I would not be contained. So, with the one woman I had at my disposal, I commenced to design a plan to bring my *hobby craft* to me (playing the field).

Many single, lonely women seek correspondence and possibly a romantic relationship with a prisoner. We, the authors, will not assume beyond our personal knowledge as to why women choose to get involved in a romantic relationship with a prisoner. Of course, we can assume that they are lonely, want to be loved, want that attention from a man to feel needed and in control of their relationship and the satisfaction of knowing that their man is not physically cheating on them. But like we said, we will not assume beyond our personal knowledge; we will stick to the facts as we lived it.

Prison Pen-Pal sites are the meeting ground for women to meet prisoners. The prisoners know such sites are a lucrative medium to tap the emotional distress of women which could gain them a financial jackpot. Ninety-nine percent of the prisoners who place their personal ads on prison pen-pal sites have ulterior motives to manipulate their potential pen pals for some type of monetary support, whether it be in the form of having money placed on their inmate account, a quarterly package, special purchase packages, stationery and postage stamps, and/or magazines and books sent to them. It does vary, because some prisoners seek visits and having someone to call, make three-way phone calls and be their outside hands and feet, a personal secretary.

The top prison pen pal sites most well-known and utilized among prison populations are Inmate Connections, Prison Pen Pals, Write a Prisoner, Friends Beyond the Wall, Prison Inmates, Inmate Classified, but there are many others that are not so popular.

Now, this is where the heartfelt, super slick creative 250 words game play comes in. The prisoner profile ad; what women can read about the inmate and find some interest in corresponding.

On the following pages you will find profile ads that are unique, creative, and well articulated. They are the type of profile ads that are used to place on prison pen pal sites in hopes to captivate the reader's interest.

Once the woman makes the first initial contact with her introduction letter to her new pen pal, the real game of *Lockin' 'em in* begins. *Lockin' 'em in* is sometimes the biggest hurdle, but and still, it's no easy deal when it comes to *Knockin' 'em off line*.

LOCKIN' 'EM IN

Eugene L. Weems, Timothy R. Richardson

LOCKIN' 'EM IN

Lockin' 'em in is an art. It requires the ability to secure an above-average assessment of your target. It is imperative to be as accurate as you can, in order to avoid saying something in your approach that may cause your target to resist. When attempting to assess the particulars of your target's character or personality traits, you must tread cautiously.

As the approacher, you should always assume your target questions your true intentions. Therefore, you should lead with the most common assurances that ease your target's concerns; i.e., *I've been hurt, is why I'm looking for companionship. I'm not looking for financial support* (though you are, just never mention it), and the big one, *I'm only interested in writing one woman exclusively because I've never been the player type; I need something real.* You've got to kind of make it appear as though these are some things you felt needed to be put out front. That way, you bring comfort to the table before she could even address these as her own concerns. This helps to plant subliminal seeds that you just may be a man after her own heart. Even though, these aforementioned concerns are generally common to expect of any woman. Sort of like the psychic at a carnival with a crystal ball. They speak in generalizations that would convince anyone who truly wants to believe that everything the psychic says is true. Same science. So, a woman who wants to find companionship, wants to believe that every approach is as genuine as it seems.

Another very important connection that needs to be made is wisdom and compatibility. For instance, in attempting to better acquaint yourself with your target, you ask what it is your target

57

likes to do; i.e., hobbies, experiences, and even travels. If you have done similar things, share your experiences and knowledge of whatever it is. If you have not, then research the information about this hobby, place or thing. How? You *make believe*, for a better word than *lie*. You simply exaggerate your experiences doing whatever it is you've researched. Be sure to research in depth in order to exaggerate with realism. What I mean by in depth is, if your target has mentioned being to Japan and shopping at a particular store, you could research the store, the area, the streets surrounding it, the route from a certain hotel in the area, local restaurants and even some of the dishes on their menus.

Why? Because this is a job. It's called *Long Con*. Some people work back-breaking jobs all day, then come home sore, tired, and sometimes injured. But the long con man sits in the comforts of his luxuries he has hustled and studies his prey, strategically planning his next move. But if he is good and chooses his moves wisely, he could win big. It's all in picking the right table to play and then playing your cards right. (see Introduction letters) These are actual letters that were used to peak the curiosity or interests of some of the most skeptical of women. They are the type of introduction letters that are composed as bait for the catch.

There are times when a woman will procrastinate in replying to your introduction letter. When this occurs after providing her a reasonable amount of time to write back (two to three weeks), a follow-up letter is sent. This letter is designed to reintroduce the possibilities that caught her attention from the beginning and get her focus back on you. Such letters are uniquely composed to stir up the *awe factor* emotions, feed her spirit with positive and inspiring desires of meeting a new friend that she could profit with happiness from his passions.

Also, the *Go Boy* factor. The *Go Boy* factor is the information you provided in your letter that says although you are in a bad situation, you continue to shoot for goals. So when a woman doesn't write back after you sent an introduction, we send what we call a *re-booster introduction letter*. This normally works every time.

(See re-booster introduction letters)

Eugene L. Weems, Timothy R. Richardson

PROFILE ADS

Eugene L. Weems, Timothy R. Richardson

John Doe

Thank you for taking the time out to recognize and accept my friend request. You must be informed that I am truly and innocently unfamiliar with the mechanics of social networking pages. Well to be frank, I am unfamiliar with the Internet altogether. Never been the tech-savvy type. My name is John Doe. I am a distinguished gentleman of mature age looking to make a friend that I could enjoy conversations with that two educated people could appreciate. I enjoy discussions about politics, and the law that govern our land. I haven't taken a bar exam, but I have on my own practiced law for almost 30 years. Let's just call it, home studies. I am a native of Cuba raised up in Puerto Rico. I am fluent in 4 languages; Latin, Spanish, Swahili and English. I speak them all equally well and could enjoy intelligent conversations in either language. Please excuse the fading of my photograph, it was taken in 2005. I've never been the photogenic type. I hope you are not of a judgmental nature, but if you are, I only hope you judge me solely by the content of my character and personality. That you would also be able to associate with me based on the caliber of my intelligence. I honestly only hope that not only could we be Internet friends, but someday become real friends that could appreciate mature discussions over the phone, or exchange letters sharing thoughts and ideas the old fashion way through the good ol' postal service. So until we reach the next phase of being "friends" I'll be here while you're there, unless you choose to meet me in the middle.

Snail Mail Address

John Doe

"I'm 2,758 miles from home and I'm lonely"

My name is John Doe and I can promise you this ad is like no other. Am I financially secure? No! Can I offer you the moon and stars? No! But I can offer you my ear to listen and my heart & mind to learn from all you have experienced in life.

I'm not looking for a wife, I have 2 years left on my sentence and I'm searching for that one jewel we all look for...A true friend! My aspirations are simple, I want to further my education through college and earn a degree in business management. I'm looking for someone who is positive in nature, I've been surrounded by negativity since I was 19. Violence, dis-respect, and lack of humility is the norm around here.

I need to be taken away from this place by corresponding with those who will help elevate me to where I know I will make it back in a place that I took for granted so many years ago.

I'm from Staten Island and to be honest I miss riding the S.I. Ferry and playing in the snow with my family. I have my high school diploma and A few trades under my belt and God willing I can make some new, true and life long friends with this ad. I'm searching for your help and please know, I'm serious! I'll be paroling to the Sacramento area in early 2014 and I'd like to parole with a P.H.D. Can you help?

Snail Mail Address

John Doe

Welcome, my name is John Doe. I'm a 56 year old distinguished gentleman of Bakersfield, California. I'm generally a very private but sincere man. Social but careful person that's known for my protective nature when it comes to my friends and family. I raised 3 daughters that are all very responsible and successful adult women today. So, I guess it's fair to say, I've done my job, and now I can share myself with a woman of my interest. To meet someone through the internet is something new to me, so I hope I'm not putting myself in a position of vulnerability. You know, being on a pen-pal site and not being chosen. I'm interested in meeting a friend that I could possibly find a lot in common with. I am also not opposed to something a little more sincere and inmate. I'm a mature man, looking for a mature woman who also wants something real.
If that woman could be you, feel free to write me at

Snail Mail Address

John Doe

I write this short letter in hopes of seeking a friend. If you're reading this page you already have interest. Let me make you famous with the mail man, because i do enjoy writing. By the way my name is John Doe, my friends call me John. I'm 38 years old, 180 pounds, 5'8" tall and built very well, brown skin, brown eyes. My hair is short with waves with a goatee. Right now in life i am single, looking for that special someone. I have a serious demeanor when it comes to relationships, I've been hurt before and i wish that on no one. I'm honest because honesty is the best policy in any relationship. Games are for children, i don't play them, and i wish not to have them played on me.

I appreciate honesty, loyalty and trust, Even if it hurts, the truth heals better than lies, if your that special someone Holla!

I am as you have read an incarcerated bachelor. Yes! I'm in prison for making bad choices and the ultimate decision is this result trying to have money, it cost me my freedom and i have accepted full responsibility for my actions. I did this to myself and it hurts, i will be lying to myself and to you if i said it didn't hurt. I'm only human and I'm paying for my mistake. So if you find interest in this page get back at me. God Bless!

Race Don't matter.

Snail Mail Address

John Doe

First off to introduce myself, my name is John though ones who are closest to me call me "John Doe." I'm a young 27 year old currently in the position that I consider to be an unfortunate one. But none the less A real grown man must take responsibility for his own actions. Feel me? Irregardless of my incarceration, I'm still a human being an even though my life may be on pause for now, I still exist and posses the attributes that make me feel alive.

But why not take it a bit further. Contemplaten' on my release I think I'd like to be involved and in touch with the outside world. With that said my set intentions are to meet A woman that I can talk to and possibly relate with. Maybe share and compare things that are or aren't of the importance to each others life in general. I'm a very open minded individual and an easy going type of guy. Interesting? I believe so when it comes to music, sports, tattoo'n, etc. Just some of the topics at hand but also to be in touch with one who likes to laugh and smile and knows how to put people in good moods. Ya know?

So if you are feelin' this brief intro then feel free to holla at me. Maybe then we can get at each other on a personal level and get to know one another a bit better. So in close....

> "Its open game/ time for me to establish what were here to gain/ feel no pain and feel no strain and fair exchange for your name/ conversation's just let it flow/ and opportunities don't let them go."

> With respect's....

John Doe

Greetings,
My name is John Doe. I am 29 years old 6'3 and 215 pounds. I would consider myself to be very physically fit, but I'm not satisfied yet. I do have tattoos that cover from about my elbows to the middle of my back (non-racial.)
I'm pushing eleven years in prison so far and about to hit my halfway point. The activities I do in my spare time are working out, studying the Bible and working as an electrician.
I would say I have an optimistic outlook on life and have a wonderful sense of humor given my current housing conditions. I am also in a sense very reclusive, but yet outgoing too.

Snail Mail Address

Click HERE mail this inmate

John Doe

Hello Ladies,

First and foremost, I'm incarcerated!

(S.B.M.) seeking a pen-pal with an open mind. Someone understanding to my present situation. I'm not looking for any financial gain nor am I into playing any games. I feel that needed to be expressed up front.

My name is John, I'm 46 a Scorpio 5'7 185 pounds, my photo speaks for itself. According to CDCR my release date is 03-12-2013. I'm single at the moment mainly because woman tend to either shy from us incarcerated men figuring we're only out to trick them out of something or abandon us for being incarcerated. In both cases, we're projected as the bad guy. However, were humans with feelings and desires to be graced with the presence of the opposite sex.

What I adore about a woman, A refined woman age range: 35-55 career minded, respectfully classy, educated, color/race doesn't matter. Although tall slender woman are most appealing to me. (No exclusions.) I like humor at times, I respect social skills. Basically, a mature woman with a bit of patience.

Snail Mail Address

John Doe

Welcome Visitor!

Have you heard any good jokes lately? Well, I'm no comedian but I'm sure if you chose any other page besides this one for your corresponding pleasure, I'm almost certain you can get a laugh out of some of those ridiculous introductions presented by some of the men on these sites. You know laced with big intelligent words, sounding like Malcom X, or College professors. I'm not putting them down at all, I'm just pickin' you up to what their putting down. I'm the real deal. No artificial flavor, no preservatives, no saturated fat, I'm all athletic muscular build, no liar, no fake.

Good man on the inside and out. Just what your family and friends would want you to have.

My name? John Doe but please call me "John." My case? Robbery. I would blame it on the rain, could blame it on Oakland, Ca. But as I said, I'm no liar. It's all my fault. I was looking for the easy way to the top. I've learned a lot though, because now I know that everything in life is earned, and if it isn't mine, to not touch it. I'm trying to earn the respect of new friends, and hopefully one day, have a woman of my very own to share my life with. So if you're looking for a man of un-cut truths and sincerity, or a lil fixer-upper of your own,

can we be friends?

If you're the truth, sincere, and real, you can reach me at:

John Doe

Hello future Pen-Pal...My name is John Doe...My friends and family call me John. I'm 51-years old and i definitely don't look like it nor do i feel like it either... I take pride in keeping myself physically, emotionally, and mentally fit... I'm 5-feet 11-inches tall and i weigh 200 pounds solid...I have a nice complexion, I have a dark brown skin, and brown eyes and a clean shaved bald head with goatee... At this moment in my life it would be a privilege to meet a beautiful woman who i could correspond with as a pen-pal friend; someone who would be willing to share and trust their lives with me a man who values and most definitely respects the feelings of others...with that said allow me to give you a little breakdown of myself, when it comes down to living my life, lets just say that I live life to the fullest and those people who are a part of my life always seem to love me because I am very open and honest...

I'm very open minded and I speak what I'm feeling... I enjoy working out, listening to all kinds of music, reading...but most importantly I enjoy the relationship I have with God, If I have nothing or no one, I can always count on him to always be there for me...I am not a religious fanatic who forces their beliefs on someone. I'm currently incarcerated and I'm paying for my mistakes and I blame nobody but myself for being locked up... Prison can either help you or destroy you, and for me it has help me to grow as a man, see myself for who I was and help to make changes I need in my life if I ever wanted to have a life and be loved by someone...What I'm seeking in a pen-pal is someone who has a strong will to want to do for themselves and others...Someone with strong self esteem and a beautiful inner beauty...Someone who loves themselves for who they are as a person...Someone who still dreams and enjoys living life to the fullest...someone who is able to be loyal, honest and respectful... Someone who isn't controlling, demanding, considers the feelings of others... Someone who places family and life in it's proper perspective... Friendship is always the beginning of something special and thats what I'm looking for, a special friend... Someone who i can share my hopes and dreams with...

Your race nor your weight matter to me only your heart and soul... If we should be the grace of God become future pen-pals you can always count on me to be here for you when nobody else will be...

John Doe

Glad to have you visit my page. My name is John Doe, a native of Louisiana, New Orleans to be exact. I fell by way of Oakland, Cali. I suppose that's where i adopted some of the not-so-popular choices that landed me here.

Obviously you're not the judgemental type or you would not have given a Pen-Pal site two clicks of the mouse. Either way, It's nice to know that good people believe in mis-steps, mistakes and misfortunes.

Are you my new friend? I sure hope so, because i find myself at a slight dis-advantage already, not being able to meet you like any other man who would want to get to know you.

Let's hope that i could meet some of the qualities you're looking for in a friend, a man, and dare i say, a lover? Please understand, that being on a Pen-Pal web site is not easy for me to be comfortable with, minus some embarrassment.

The embarrassment is driven by the potential of rejection; yeah, I'm just as human as anyone else, I want to be accepted and make friends, even in my unfortunate situation. So yes, it would be refreshing to meet someone new, and introduce myself to the dating world again. I'm absent from being free, not from being a gentlemen.

I'm just waiting for a women to let me. Is that wrong? I'm a very mature gentlemen, open-minded, and a compassionate person by nature.

I'm Looking to correspond with a woman who just might wanna' experience and make new and pleasant memories of life, love and laughter.

I'd love to hear from you and promise to respond to every letter sent. Take care of yourself and I'll do the same.

Foreal,

John Doe

I'm looking for someone to connect with me on more levels than one. I'm 43 years old, and know what I want. I know what I am, and admire my values. I've spent years of my life fine tuning my slight imperfections, and learning from my mistakes to make the necessary corrections.
So after spending the needed time to fix myself, complete my soul searching, and understanding exactly who I am and what my aspirations and goals are; I am confident and ready to offer myself up to be shared and appreciated by a like mind.
I would like to correspond with a woman that I could have a spiritual as well as intellectual connection with. I want to share myself unconditionally with a woman with a good and fair heart, understanding mind, and possibly a good spiritual woman who looks to find the good and decency in all. Are you the one that has been inspired to share your story with me? All things happen for a reason. Could your reading this be a reason for us to happen?
I sure hope so.

Snail Mail Address

Eugene L. Weems, Timothy R. Richardson

INTRODUCTION LETTERS

Eugene L. Weems, Timothy R. Richardson

INTRODUCTION LETTER

Dear (Name)

Though I am truly surprised that you decided to open the door to correspond with me and allow me an opportunity to introduce myself, I have to admit that I am honestly embarrassed.

Your profile is that of such a beautiful woman of confidence and pride that I almost decided not to respond. Why? Because everything about your look says you would never give me the time of day. Well, I suppose either looks can be deceiving or you're as beautiful on the inside as you are outside. It's not often that I am not judged solely on my looks alone. My bark is bigger than my bite.

I pay for a service to monitor my MySpace page because I currently have no access to the Internet, and I intended to find a real friend, not just another image on my page, so thank you so much for being open and down-to-earth real and genuine.

There is so much I'd like to tell you about myself that I don't know where to begin. I suppose the beginning is best, huh? Well, here goes.

I was born in (town, state) on (month, date, year). My parents went their own separate ways when I was (age) old. I went with my (mother/father) to (state). This is where I grew up in a not-so-nice neighborhood surrounded by all that you can imagine in an east or west (city) ghetto. I grew up to a learned behavior that to be a hustler or drug dealer was the only way I could earn respect or even survive. Yes, of course I understand now that those are only the choices made by people unwilling to be responsible or accountable for their actions.

So, because of my poor choices, I'm finishing up a debt that I owe to a society that deserves to have one more productive member within it, and one less destructive member. And now I have (years/months) remaining before I'm released, after being sentenced to (years/months). I have truly learned lessons that will stick with me for life.

When I was out, I (your accomplishments) that exposed me to talents that I had no idea I even possessed. Since I've been away, I've been rehabilitating myself to learn new behaviors that can be admired and respected.

I acquired a college credited certificate in business communication, business math, different software programs, office services, filing and more. I co-authored a book currently being edited and prepared for release early next year.

I've designed an urban clothing line that I would like to see become a brand someday. And just in general, I have finally grown up to a point of recognizing that I am the only person who has been in my own way.

Finally thinking outside the box and trying to realize my maximum potential. In discovering these wonderful attributes about myself, I now realize that I must surround myself with positive people, like-minded people, and encouraging friends with genuine positive advice.

Oh my goodness! (name of person), please forgive me for rambling on so long about myself, but I have to say that I'm not used to having to introduce myself like this, so I'm a little nervous. I wish I could have met you under different circumstances, even invited you to a glass of white or red wine at a jazz lounge, or even to a lunch like any other person in the free world, and discuss current events and the latest *breaking news* and how either sad or exciting it might be.

I don't perceive you as the judgmental type because you definitely would not have allowed me to write to you, but I still wish I could somehow make you feel welcome and comfortable. This is why I felt compelled to open myself up like so, that way you can know all about me.

Please feel free to ask me any question that you wish. (name), my life is an open book. At least one thing I can offer as a friend is an abundance of honesty, if only you choose to respond and keep correspondence with me.

I would like to show your heart where my heart is, and hope that somewhere or somehow you could find a compatibility that might encourage a friendship.

By the way, I've never heard of (city, town, state), so what metro city are you near?

And if I'm not too nosy in asking, what is it that you do for a living? If I'm out of order for asking, please forgive me and just ignore that question. I don't mean to get too personal; I'm only trying to make conversation with hopefully a new positive friend.

Are you religious or no? What's your Zodiac sign? What type of music do you like?

Myself, well, I enjoy all sorts. I like some country, R&B soul, some soft rock, jazz, very little reggae, and some rap. And lately I've been getting into the newer pop music. My favorite food is seafood, though I could just die for a really decent spinach salad with a raspberry vinaigrette dressing with crushed walnuts and mandarin orange slices.

Sorry, getting hungry just thinking about the simple pleasures one denies himself when he's serving time.

I enjoy exercise, writing, reading, traveling, dressing nice, smelling good and skiing and horseback riding.

I used to go to Half Moon Bay and pay to rent for rides on the horses they have off of Highway 92.

I learned to ski through a sports training program in Yerington and Carson, Nevada.

What is it that you enjoy? What makes you laugh to the point of tears? Care to share any of your fears? Am I the first man in prison you've ever made a friend with?

Ya know, I sure hope you can respect my honesty and are willing to continue on this journey of friendship and correspondence with me. I'm sure it is so much I can learn from you, advice you could share with me, and overall show me how to be comfortable with myself in all the new changes I've made for myself. I have (years/months) left here, and I would like to utilize the remainder of my time sharing more of myself, my goals and my ideals with you.

Why? Because being in this situation can be somewhat lonely and depressing at times, and everybody needs somebody to talk to. Can my somebody be you? I sure hope so.

Sorry if I took up too much of your time with such a long letter, but I was just happy to have a new friend.

Hope to hear from you soon.

If you send photos, I'll send you some of me.

Your new friend,

(your name)

p.s. I decided to enclose a photo I had taken before my arrest. Hopefully, you like it. It's yours to keep if you wish to correspond, but if you decide not to continue correspondence and have no desire to have my photo, please return it. But I sure hope you decide to keep it, and me, as a friend.

INTRODUCTION LETTER

Dear (name),

I open this letter with respect and hopes to meet a new friend today. That my words will be reason for your smile. And your curiosity of me will be the beginning to meeting someone wonderful and special.

As much as I would love to make acquaintance with you under ordinary circumstances, ya know, shopping mall, restaurant, college campus, or a festival like a free man, my current situation excludes that possibility. But just as well, I have to say, "The pleasure of knowing your name is all mine."

My name is John Doe. I'm a man of many talents and aspirations. I'm down to earth, ambitious, sincere, friendly and a fun person to be around. How about you? Meeting under these extraordinary circumstances does not mean at all that we can't come together like two normal people meeting anywhere else. And what has motivated me to compose this letter from the start was that my boy said you were interested in meeting someone, so I wanted to say hello and let you know I exist.

My heart is big and easy. I'm looking for someone loyal, of substance, open-minded, ambitious, comforting, and loves to laugh, as these are some of my interests as well. I'm attracted to positivity and distance from drama, which I feel promote the growth and development of a deep and meaningful friendship. I'm motivated to travel the journeys that pen, paper and conversation may take us.

Any and all subjects are open. The only strings are the ones we both agree on. I'm not concerned with physical descriptions because I search for true beauty that's beyond eye's view, that can only be found within.

I have no kids, and I do not use drugs or smoke.

Well, there is much to learn about me. I will be looking to hear from you. You take care, and write soon.

Sincerely,
John Doe

INTRODUCTION LETTER

Dear (name)

Finally, I have a chance to reach beyond these walls that confine me! Please do excuse me while I stretch my fingers out, exhaling words of praise and appreciation to you for giving me an outlet to be heard beyond the bondage that has silenced me.

You have no idea how easy it is to be forgotten when you're in prison. Guys like myself are all reaching out for even the remotest slice of freedom they can find, even if it's through pen and paper. Bonus if she ends up being as beautiful as your profile is.

Again, I could never thank you enough for treating lonely old (name) like an equal. My hat is off to you, my lady. Salute!

Anyways, my gratitude extended, I would like to better introduce myself.

My name is (name). I am (age) years old, born (date of birth), so yeah, (age) is just around the corner. Feeling just as young as I did at 22, so I'm living proof that age is just a number. Truth!

Anyways, I have to admit that I do have some genuine concerns for you and your loved ones being in tornado/hurricane season out there. I'm unfamiliar with the geography out your way, so I'm curious of how often a city like (name) is in serious danger. Are you worried? I hope you'll be okay. I don't know if you're a religious person or not, but I am, so I'll keep you in my prayers, 'kay?

So, I know you're curious about how I was able to message you through MySpace. Com? Well, I pay a company that mediates social networking pages for inmates to maintain ties to the free world, and I pay per response to messages. Hence, requesting your mail address to miss the middleman fee to the company.

So again, thank you for your understanding. Now, to answer a few questions I'm sure you must have.

My charge is (xxx). My sentence is (years). My release date (date). So yeah, I have less than a year left here paying my debt to society.

What have I learned? Plenty! I mostly have come to finally understand that fast money lacks two major things. (1) It doesn't amount to the worth of serving prison time; and (2) fast money gotten is even faster money gone!

So this experience has been full of priceless lessons learned, and so many losses that the punishment was more than (years/months). And so far, one thing falling in my favor, finally, is you not judging me, but instead allowing my voice an exit.

I'm also glad you accepted my friends request, which means you were able to view my photos. I'm curious, whaddya think? I'm (nationality), very small portion of (nationality), but being African American, I am wondering if you've been in any kind of relationship with a black man?

If the question has made you uncomfortable in any way, please accept my apology, and just ignore my forward approach. But you appear to be an absolutely beautiful woman and I just want to know you, all about you, what it is that makes you laugh to the point of tears, what makes you sad, what's your favorite food, animal, color, and just totally, exactly who is this beautiful womanly creation named Ms. (name).

I've love to share all of me with you. Why you? Well, first and most important of all, because knowing my situation, you did not judge me, ignore me, or deny me just based on me being in prison.

You've helped me to realize that beautiful women are not all with their noses snubbed at those who make mistakes, or like me, who have fallen and have to dust myself off and try once again to join everyone else. I haven't been completely "in the way" during my (age) years on this planet. I've accomplished a few admirable goals I'm somewhat proud of, like for instance:

1)

2)

3) Since I've been incarcerated here, this time, I've completed a college course in office services, business communications, business math and several other certificates I can actually use in the free world in the next (xxx) months. So by no means (name) do I have any plans to fail, because I have not failed to plan! I'm all over it this time around.

So, I had a thought. Since you have seen photos of me, and can even copy them from the internet if you wish, would it be too much to ask if you could send me pictures of yourself to really see who it is that I'm wanting to write to so badly?

You don't mind if I make you famous with the mailman, do you? Because I can keep the letters coming to you if you respond to this one, beautiful lady of my desire.

In case I've failed to mention my origin, inmate from (city/state). I intend to parole to (city, California) when I leave here, just get away from the drama filled environment I've grown so accustomed to. Ya know, change of scenery, change of pace, change of everything. Even a change of the type of people I surround myself with. I plan on going about two hours outside of Seattle to a town named (name) where crime is low and drama is next to none.

Whoa, sorry about rambling on for so long. I told you there was much I wanted to share with you, so I'll save some in case you write me back. I'll be looking forward to your letter, and hopefully some pictures of yourself.

Until then, take care of yourself. Watch out for tornados, and don't forget about the little people in California prison, like me (smile).

Sincerely, your friend,

(name)

THE TALKING LETTER

Why, thank you! It feels good to get out of that cold, dark, smothered and cramped envelope...not to mention, free at last! Has anyone ever told you that your hands are sooo soft and that you have a light touch? Can I ask a favor? Can you hold me up and let me see how the free world looks, because I was in a dark place, and trust me, anything other than this place gots to be better!

Niiice. You have a very beautiful home, not to mention your beautiful smile.

I'm sure you've noticed the return address on the envelope stamped STATE PRISON GENERATED MAIL. Please, be a sweetheart and don't let this detour you from getting to know the person that sent me. He came across your address and liked what he read about you. At first, he was somewhat hesitant to write because he had traveled that road of disappointment before and was pretty much afraid of being disappointed once again. Anyhow, I told him to go for it and take a chance. You know the saying...one can only try.

Oh, by the way, I am The Talking Letter, and my sole purpose in creation was to bring a smile to your face and express one's true inner feelings. Yes, one's inner thoughts and one's desires. Right now, his inner thought and true intent is to get to know you and become friends. Everyone needs someone special in their life, a person they can be open and honest with, without being judged. He's an okay guy, with a good heart. He holds loyalty, honesty and understanding above all things, and if given the opportunity, I promise that you will not regret your decision. Unlike him, I am free, not to mention in your presence.

If I may ask you one more favor? May I have a hug? It really would be nice to be held in the arms of someone special. Although I'm just a letter, I have feelings, too!

By the way, my sender's name is John Doe, a handsome (xxx), nice physique, who has been on this earth for (xxx) years. He has many talents, but a writer and poet by trade. He loves to read powerfully written books. I believe he's reading "United We Stand" by Eugene L. Weems. A very heartfelt read. He does also recommend that you read it and let him know what you have to say about it. You can learn more about the book on www.Amazon.com.

Also, feel free to ask him any questions your heart desires, for he has nothing to hide. Oh, yeah, before I forget, he said to smile, because that's what he was doing when he stuffed me into the envelope.

Write him back, even if it's just to say hello, okay?

Your friend,

The Talking Letter

INTRODUCTION LETTER

Hi (name);

Happy Holidays. How's my friend? I hope all is well with you and your family. I was just thinking about you and felt compelled to write. To be honest, I have never stopped thinking about you since receiving your first letter. Sometimes I catch myself staring at this photo of you, lost in a fantasy of us (smiling). I am so excited to learn more about you.

This next letter I write will require you to be sitting in the bathtub filled with warm soapy water, with candles providing the only light, and one of your favorite slow jams to create the right mood as you read my letter. But before I'm able to compose such a letter and fulfill my motive, I will need a letter from you telling me about your desires and pleasures. So if you come through, then I'll *cum* through you (smiling).

Moving along, before I start getting excited, how was your holiday? (name), I want to know everything there is to know about you, your favorite foods, colors, books, movies, *positions!* Your dislikes, fears, and the things that motivate you to be great. The reason why I would like to know these things, 'cause I'm on a quest to see to it that I fill every aspect and every void in your life, so that you feel complete and experience contentment. That is my mission, and the more you get to know me, the quicker you'll realize that I put 360% into everything I do. So rest assured that I will replace your fears with confidence and reliance in me. I intend to, if you'll allow me, to replace your dislikes with approbations and favor. Remove all that discourages you, and propel you toward success. I intend on being your motivation, always respecting and considering the well-being of you and the people you love.

So you see (name), you have hit the jackpot with me, and if you are ready for the most exciting and fulfilling adventure of your life, then strap up and ride with me. You will not be disappointed. It's all about you!

Well, listen, I'm not going to write much more today, but I want you to keep this letter and maintain it as if it was a promissory note to assure the contents I've conveyed become reality.

Until I hear from you, may life treat you and your family like the treasures you are. With that I remain, sincerely,

John Doe

INTRODUCTION LETTER

(Name),

Your letter reached my presence with you in thought, your written words came to me in a time of need, when I needed a reason to bring a smile to my face, and I must say that you are that reason for my high spirit and big smile. Thank you for making a difference in my world that most of the time seems so cloudy and overwhelming. Today, you are my angel. The angel I hope someday would become to have a great meaning into my life and share a part of my world that is special to me.

The more I take the opportunity to sit and compose my string of words to you, I feel that I could share a part of me that I have been so reluctant to do with anyone else. Your aura and honesty from your letters tells me a great deal about you. It says to me, you are kind and good hearted, loving and needing to be loved in return. That's the vibe I get from you, and if you were to tell me I have it all wrong, then I would not believe you, because God doesn't lie. That's one of the many gifts that He has blessed me with, perception, and I perceive you to be a beautiful person and I'm sure with time our friendship will blossom like a mass of flowers into a long lasting, meaningful and special friendship.

I don't recall telling you this, but I am a very passionate man. These walls tend to hinder the true identity of a person's heart, and under such conditions, it compels me to adopt a more firm and demanding personality that becomes dense and limited only to this world that I live in. although I have been able to keep the real me separated from the mask that I choose to wear behind these walls. It has been quite some time since I had the opportunity and the feeling of someone worthy to share the real me with. You have the key that has opened the flood gates to something more than exciting, loving and enchanting to a human soul. You have allowed me to be who I am. That is a fulfillment to the spirit and I hope that I am capable of fulfilling your spirit with a part of me that is pure as the blue sky and honest as the air that you breathe daily.

I hope to hear from you soon. Until the next meeting of our pen and paper, you take care.

Sincerely,

(name)

INTRODUCTION LETTER

Dear Ms. Lady;

It was a pleasant surprise to receive a letter from you today. You sound like a true down to earth and gentle woman who I would really like to share time with, either writing letters to or sitting with in the visiting room here, enjoying lunch, laughs and maybe even occasional hugs and kisses, if you're lucky. Just kidding... I meant to say, if I'm lucky (smile)! I hope you really are smiling. At least I don't have to tell you that I do have a great sense of humor. I hope you do, as well. A few other things I should tell you are the answers to your questions:

1) Why am I here?

(crime) Why? Because I grew up in (city) and life was hard, and my choices were few and my understanding was blurry. I don't make excuses for my poor choices. I have since that time learned from them. So no, I am not mad at society for enforcing the law. I am only grateful that I do have a chance to try again at having a normal life on the right track.

2) When do I go home?

My release date is (date). I have a bit less than (months) away. That gives me some quality time to learn more about myself, and any woman that wants to learn more about me and be part of my life while I'm at my growing point. I would appreciate a courageous woman of that faith in a real man accepting responsibility for his actions and/or errors.

3) Where would I like my life to go afterwards?

To the moon, Alice! Just kidding. (that was from the Honeymooners)

Seriously, I want what every man wants; a woman that accepts me for me, loves me unconditionally, allows me to feel comfortable and confident in the skin I'm in, trusts me to do my very best to protect her, provide for her and do her very best to support me in whatever it is I can or am doing to the best of my ability. I am just a man!

4) If you're curious about what I want in a woman, well, are you sitting down, because this list will be at least 42 pages. Here goes! Ha-ha! (smile)

Okay, okay, I'll get serious. Such a kidder when I'm nervous.

Anyways, the question. I only expect a woman to be honest, pure, put into a relationship everything that she expects to get out of it. I'm a great listener and expect for her to be just as considerate.

5) Overall, what kind of person do I consider myself to be?

Well, my mother raised me to e a gentleman who cares for and provides for those he loves. I'm a strong but gentle spirit, kind, but serious, friendly, but my no means a pushover, sweet but far from soft, sincere and honest, sometimes to a fault. I've been alone for quite some time and would love to share the quiet company of a woman once again. It's so nice to be acquainted with a woman again after so very long.

Maybe one of these weekends we could sit and talk. It would be nice, if I could ever be so lucky. But just in case you could be so real, enclosed is a visiting form to mail back, if you wish. Even a photo would be nice. I'm looking for someone to connect with me on more levels than one. I'm (xxx) years old and know what I want. I know who I am and admire my values. I've spent (xxx) years of my life fine tuning my slight imperfections and learning from my mistakes to make the necessary corrections, so after spending and understanding exactly who I am and what my aspirations and goals.

I am now confident and ready to offer myself up to be shared and appreciated by a like mind. I would like to correspond with a woman that I could have a spiritual as well as intellectual connection with. I want to share myself unconditionally with a woman with a good and fair heart, a woman who looks to find the good and decency in all. Are you the one that has been inspired to share your story with me?

All things happen for a reason. Could your reading this be a reason for us to happen? I sure hope so. My name is John Doe. It's your choice what category you'd like to be recognized in.

Sincerely,
John Doe

RE-BOOSTER INTRODUCTION LETTERS

A follow-up letter that is sent after two to three
weeks with no response to an introduction letter.
The re-booster introduction is designed to
re-introduce the possibilities that originally caught
her attention.

Eugene L. Weems, Timothy R. Richardson

RE-BOOSTER INTRODUCTION

First and Foremost,

Greetings to you, dear new lady of my interest. Yeah, I'm reaching out once more for two reasons: (1) I haven't received a response from my first letter that I sent in response to your original email to Incarcerated Bachelors-Pen-Pals.com, so I'm not sure if you've even received my first letter. And (2) I'm also not sure if I expressed how very appreciative I am for you to acknowledge my existence.

Please allow me to show you where my heart is. I suppose you may be busy with the daily activities of life and the responsibilities that govern adulthood, so I don't expect you to write as much as I would like to write to you. But only if you will let me, I intend to make you famous with the mailman, because if you invite me into your circle of friendship, or just your acquaintance, I can see me writing to you every day. Let's just say it's the attention of a woman alone that motivates me, and the fact that you chose to open a door for us to get to know each other better; you inspired me to want to share myself again. Just when I began to categorize all women as the same, you know, (forget those of us in prison), as if not every human is entitled to make mistakes, some more consequential than others, but and still, babe, I'm not perfect, nor ever pretended to be. I'm only me. But hey, I don't want this to be uncomfortable for you if you've chosen not to correspond with me after all and I'm the last to find out that's your decision. So, in case you don't respond, I'll make this my last letter so that you don't feel harassed by continuous letters from a prisoner, but now and forever treat yourself like royalty and never forget, women are the greatest wonder of the world and I'm ever so grateful to have been noticed by you.

Sincerely,

RE-BOOSTER INTRODUCTION

Dear (name),

First of all, I hope this letter reached you at a time in your life when all is well and hopefully you're even in the mood to hear from me one last time. But now, if the truth is all you're interested in hearing, that suits me just fine, because... well, ya see, the truth is, that I'm just not sure what to do in this here situation. I don't know if you're looking for me to show you a little persistence and pursue my interests in you or to bug off. I'm honestly confused.

Because, from my understanding, you sent me a message including your address. I took that to mean you wanted to learn more about me as a person, me as a man, and to open a dialogue between the two of us. Please forgive me if I misunderstood, and besides, the last thing I want to do is appear desperate or harassing.

So again, forgive me if I am intruding on your personal space or time. Being that this is my last attempt at proving my persistence and sincerity, I figure I'd better make this one count. *They* say you never get a second chance to make a good first impression, but since we don't know who *they* are, let's both prove *them* wrong and go forward...can we?

Let me start fresh and re-introduce myself.

Hello there (name). please call me (name). I am so embarrassed by my presentation, so please excuse me for inviting you into a space in my life that is in such disarray. Ya know, prisoner and all. Wish I could invite you to a comfortable seat and say *Make yourself feel at home,* offer you something to drink and talk about current events and the latest breaking news development and how either sad or exciting it may have been.

Simple things that many of us incarcerated men had taken for granted until that opportunity no longer existed. The smallest of womanly pleasures and just enjoying the presence or attention of the opposite sex is no longer a privilege I will take for granted ever again. When I received your address, I thought I found a friend I could be a listener and supporter to, ya know, a friend for real, or who knows?

But either way, I felt I owed you my gratitude for choosing to be the woman to let this genie out of the bottle to grant some wishes. And since I, like any make-believe genie, have three wishes to grant, I only hope that your requests of me would all be well thought out, considerate, and would encourage me to keep going in the positive direction I'm focused on at this point in my life. I'm no psychic, but I'm sure you have some questions similar to the following that I'll be providing answers to, so here goes:

Q) How did I find myself trapped in a bottle?

A) Hanging around some "not-so-nice genies" and casting spells for profitable gain. But seriously, running with a faulty crows and cutting corners to get the quick money.

Q) Why do I feel I need to grant wishes? (Why change?)

A) Because, for one, I've matured; and secondly, because I intend to begin doing as much positive as possible to create balance and harmony for the error of my past behaviors.

Q) If you let out of my bottle to claim as y our own personal genie or man servant, how do you know that I've changed from the "not-so-nice genie" of the past to the "gentle genie" of today?

A) Because now I've learned so much, and I can offer you an abundance of truth and honesty if only you would put even a smidgen of faith in me. I dare not disappoint. Let's just say, I promise to treat as fragile your heart if you let me hold it, or even as a friend, let me view it from afar. Let me investigate your style, let me learn your smiles, honest or just polite, a sneer or even contrite, let me know you some.

If you're extra guarded, let me share with you a bit about me. Of course, a saint I ain't. (I know it's poor grammar), but again I say, a saint I ain't! I'm just being down to earth honest since this is *my last attempt* at trying to know you. I feel you deserve to know everything about the man you'll choose to grant a personal invite into your life, or even the man you'll choose to ignore. In case you choose to ignore me instead, at least I'll know I was sincere in my approach and you can hopefully still appreciate my honesty and surrender.

Why am I alone in prison, good looking guy like myself? Well, *Karma.* What goes around, comes around. Yeah, there was a time I broke a heart or two. I've had girlfriends, played the field before, even thought I had Mrs. Right once, but when I tried to be Mr. Right, all that I did prior to finding who I thought to be Mrs. Right came back around to bite me back. Yeah, I wasn't smiling then. Having my heart broken was the worst thing to ever happen to me, and now I'm somewhat careful who I let inside nowadays.

I do understand, though, that one woman does not define all women, so I'm' going to try again one day, but for now, a friend to share my thoughts, fears, joys and ideas with will do just fine.

Yeah, by the way, I'm somewhat religious, so I do thank God for small favors and the big ones, too.

Small favor: being able to express myself to a woman again.

Big favor: well, duh! You, of course. Thank God!

Happy to write. Can we be friends? If so, what do we do first, friend?

Never had a real friend, so what's the first thing real friends do? Walk me through this. I've been bottled up for a spell, so I'm trusting you won't let me down.

I'm a believer that you read my intro on my web page for a reason, found some common interests and felt some compatibility or you wouldn't have given me your address to write to you, so I'm assuming you either misplaced my address, forgot what I look like, or never received my letters, or just have been busy with the daily rituals of living live. But I'm doing everything I can to convince myself it is not something I said or did between the moment you decided to allow me to write to you and the moment you received my first letter that turned you off completely about me.

In case you forgot why you decided to introduce yourself, please visit my page again at www.IncarceratedBachelors-PenPals.com. See you there, or at mail call h ere.

If I don't hear from you this time, I can take a hint and promise to take a hike. (smile) And hey, take good care of yourself.

Sincerely

Eugene L. Weems, Timothy R. Richardson

INCARCERATED BACHELORS

Eugene L. Weems, Timothy R. Richardson

INCARCERATED BACHELORS

I could not miss. I stepped up the game of playing the field from behind the prison walls to heights that one can only fathom. I hooked up with a friend who is an entrepreneurial genius and now the co-author of this book. We sat down at the round table and constructed a plan for our own pen pal service that was designed to attract women looking to find love, romance, friendship, or just a pen pal to correspond with. The one woman at my disposal on the outside designed the website for us (www.IncarceratedBachelors-PenPals.com). It became known as the best pen-pal service available. The only pen-pal site that screened prisoners for history of violence against women and children, or perpetrators of sex crimes. This was one thing we made sure of, not allowing any inmate who was a rapist or who had any sex crimes against women or children on our site.

Incarcerated Bachelors-Pen Pals website was depicted as an upscale pen pal company that featured deserving, handsome, hand-picked individuals that were considered to have style, class and swagger. All the men featured on the site were scheduled for release within five years or less.

This ploy encouraged women to write men on our site because they actually saw potential for something real with a man that could possibly be coming home to them. We offered website visitors the option to email their desired potential pen pals if they felt uncomfortable with snail mailing their message from their home or P.O. box address. As we learned, some women are skeptical about giving out their home address to a prisoner, as they should be, no doubt about that. (See Incarcerated Bachelors-Pen Pals website pages)

The advertising and promotion campaign we implemented to attract and lure women to the website was executed in a creative and absolutely brilliant way. We will not disclose our entire marketing strategies due to confidentiality agreements, but we will share the methods of those that we can.

I'm sure you've heard about blogging, and for those who are not familiar, blogging is a way to publish stories, letters, poetry, announcements, etc. on the Internet where it can be seen and read by anyone anywhere with a computer and Internet access. Our most successful blog posting was what we called The Oprah Winfrey Blog, which began with *OPRAH WINFREY WAS RIGHT AGAIN!*

We had my lady friend post the blog on as many blog sites as possible. The results were tremendous, as we had assumed women would come running to the Incarcerated Bachelors-Pen Pals website, if nothing more than to satisfy their curiosity. We knew that millions of women respected Oprah and took her advice, so quoting Oprah as having said, *All the good men are locked up in prison*, was all that was needed to raise the interest of women to the possibilities of finding their dream guy at Incarcerated Bachelors-PenPals.com. of course, Oprah didn't write, endorse or have anything to do with such blog. (See the Oprah Winfrey Blog)

We also posted solicitations on Craigslist website by targeting women who had posted personal ads in the Casual Encounters section. Many ads were provocative; women seeking one-night stands or a certain type of guy to be their sex partner. We would email them as well as post what we called the Craigslist Bait. (See Craigslist Bait)

You would be surprised at how many women replied and how many fell prey to this game of pimpin', playin' and mackin' for the purpose of money stackin'.

As mentioned earlier, this was not a game, but a job, a business, and it had to be conducted professionally, which it certainly was. With the overwhelming volume of letters from new women pen pals, we kept a daily correspondence logsheet for all correspondence received and sent out. This helped us remember names and dates later and became indispensible. (See Daily Correspondence Logsheet)

We also made a Business Correspondence Biography for each woman we found worthy of pursuing as a pen pal. We called it business correspondence biography because each woman was viewed as a potential source of financial gain. This logsheet is where all her personal information, including standard name and address, likes and dislikes, interests, family information, etc. The reason to collect so much information is because it's imperative that the small details are not forgotten, and this becomes your reference. You also gain brownie points with pen pals when you remember the important things about them, like what makes them happy, their childrens' birthdays, and so forth. (See Business Correspondence Biography)

Eugene L. Weems, Timothy R. Richardson

STATE OF CALIFORNIA		T.A.B.E. Score: **ABOVE 4.0**		DEPARTMENT OF CORRECTIONS

RULES VIOLATION REPORT

CDC NUMBER	INMATE'S NAME		RELEASE/BOARD DATE	INST	HOUSING NO.	LOG NO.
K64196	RICHARDSON			▇	▇	C08/11-036

VIOLATED RULE NO(S):	SPECIFIC ACTS		LOCATION	DATE	TIME
3024	BUSINESS DEALINGS BY AN INMATE		▇	8/22/2011	12:00

CIRCUMSTANCES

On August 22, 2011 at approximately 1200 hours, the ▇▇▇ Investigative Service Unit (ISU) concluded an investigation into, "Business dealing by an Inmate" being conducted by Inmate Timothy RICHARDSON (K-64196, CG-103L). Specifically, RICHARDSON owns and operates a website entitled, "Incarceratedbachelors-penpals.com" a site introducing honest, trustworthy and deserving, single men who seeks to meet someone special (see attachment #1).

A review of the website revealed ten inmates housed in ▇▇▇ Facility ▇▇ as members of the website (see attachment #2). Membership costs a total of $125.00 a year, which is sent to an address in Emeryville, California. Checks and money orders are asked to be made payable to, "T-Rich" a known moniker of RICHARDSON (see attachment #3). A review of RICHARDSON'S visiting records reveals he has several approved visitors who reside in Oakland, California located near Emeryville, who in turn may be responsible for assisting RICHARDSON operate his business.

REPORTING EMPLOYEE (Typed Name and Signature)		DATE	ASSIGNMENT	RDO'S
▶ ▇, Sergeant			ISU	

REVIEWING SUPERVISOR'S SIGNATURE	DATE	INMATE SEGREGATED PENDING HEARING	
▶ ▇, Sergeant			
		DATE	LOC

CLASSIFIED	OFFENSE DIVISION:	DATE	CLASSIFIED BY (Typed Name and Signature)	HEARING REFERRED TO
☐ ADMINISTRATIVE			▶	☐ HO ☒ SHO ☐ SC ☐ FC
☐ SERIOUS				

COPIES GIVEN INMATE BEFORE HEARING

☐ CDC 115	BY: (STAFF'S SIGNATURE)	DATE	TIME	TITLE OF SUPPLEMENT			
	▶						
☐ INCIDENT REPORT LOG NUMBER:	BY: (STAFF'S SIGNATURE)	DATE	TIME	BY: (STAFF'S SIGNATURE)		DATE	TIME
	▶			▶			

HEARING

FINDINGS

The HO finds that all time constraints and due process requirements _HAVE_ been met.
RICHARDSON was found _Guilty_ of 3024(a), for the specific act of **BUSINESS DEALINGS BY AN INMATE** an Admin offense.

DISPOSITION

RICHARDSON is assessed <u>0</u> days loss of behavioral credit consistent with a Division **"Admin"** offense.
RICHARDSON is assessed <u>30</u>days loss of Privileges, Phone From: <u>8/30/2011</u>, to: <u>9/29/2011</u>.
RICHARDSON was counseled and reprimanded.

↳ (SEE ATTACHED) ↳
Continued on pages 2 and 3

REFERRED TO ☐ CLASSIFICATION ☐ BPT/NAEA				
ACTION BY: (TYPED NAME)		SIGNATURE	DATE	TIME
▇ Sergeant		▶	8/30/11	10:30
REVIEWED BY: (SIGNATURE)	DATE	CHIEF DISCIPLINARY OFFICER'S SIGNATURE	DATE	
▶ ▇-Captain		▶ ▇ Associate Warden (A)		
☒ COPY OF CDC 115 GIVEN INMATE AFTER HEARING		BY: (STAFF'S SIGNATURE) ▶	DATE	TIME

CDC 115 (7/88)

STATE OF CALIFORNIA

DEPARTMENT OF CORRECTIONS

PAGE____OF____

RULES VIOLATION REPORT - PART C

CDC NUMBER	INMATE'S NAME	LOG NUMBER	INSTITUTION	TODAY'S DATE
K64196	RICHARDSON	C08/11-036	▬▬▬	8/22/2011

☐ SUPPLEMENTAL ☒ CONTINUATION OF: ☒ 115 CIRCUMSTANCES ☐ HEARING ☐ IE REPORT ☐ OTHER_____

Additionally, a Myspace and Facebook account managed on behalf of RICHARDSON directs guests to visit his website, "Incarceratedbachelors-penpals.com". Each of these accounts includes photographs of RICHARDSON (See attachment #4).

ISU will contact Myspace and Facebook in order to have the accounts removed, which are currently being managed on behalf of RICHARDSON. The website "Incarceratedbachelors-penpals.com" will continue to be monitored and will result in further disciplinary action should RICHARDSON'S behavior continue. Inmate RICHARDSON is aware of this report. ▬▬▬▬▬▬▬▬▬▬▬▬▬▬▬▬▬▬▬▬▬▬▬▬▬▬▬▬▬▬

SIGNATURE OF WRITER ▬▬▬ Sergeant		DATE SIGNED 8/22/2011
GIVEN BY: (Staff's Signature)	DATE SIGNED	TIME SIGNED
COPY OF CDC 115-C GIVEN TO INMATE		

109

Eugene L. Weems, Timothy R. Richardson

INCARCERATED BACHELORS

PENPALS.COM

WEB PAGES

(This gives a full layout of how the website

Looked and its content used to attract visitors)

Eugene L. Weems, Timothy R. Richardson

carcerated Bachelors

Home | About Us | Pen Pals | Contact Us | Icare | Join Here

"A website with men of style and swagger"

This site you are about to enter is designed for adults seeking prison penpals. These single men are looking for women who want to write a prisoner. Are you looking for friendship, romance, love, marriage, or to find your soul mate? These Inmate Connections can be made into Friends beyond the wall. What sets our site apart from the rest is the thorough screening process provided by our company to reassure our Web visitors that no members featured on this site are currently registered sex offenders. Our selective processing procedures allows us to choose men of Style and Swagger. This company is not profit driven. Our mission is to provide a liaison tool to combine meaningful relationships that would accomplish harmony between both the visitor and the members of this site. Your perfect match can be waiting for you.

You MUST Be 18 years of Age or older to use this site

Click Here to Enter

Incarcerated Bachelors Pen-Pal Website

"A site for those with style and swagger"

Incarcerated bachelor's is an upscale pen pal company for men who are seeking friendship, love, relationships, romance, or just a pen pal of quality.

Incarcerated Bachelors-PenPals.com was created for the very purpose of introducing honest, trustworthy, and deserving single men to classy, sexy, beautiful, wealthy women who seek to meet someone special like you.

The member's listed on this site will be thoroughly screened to ensure compatible associations.

Don't wait any longer to meet that special someone!

Get listed on the best pen-pal site out there!

www.IncarceratedBachelors-PenPals.com

Mailing Address
Incarcerated Bachelors
PO Box 99491
Emeryville, CA 94662

Member Application

<u>1-year membership</u>

~~$125.00 upon approval~~ $60.00 Summer Special
Includes:
250 words and 2 photos
Hit Counter - **Free**
Song of your choice will play during viewing of your page - **Free**

All Modifications to website - $10 each
Modifications include - Change song choice, change photos, change language of add
Additional photos - $5 per photo
Additional 50 words - $5 per 50 words

- ☐ All website visitors will have the option to email you. Emails will be mailed to you weekly.
- ☐ Your will also be featured on incarcerated bachelors' Facebook and MySpace page for **FREE**
- ☐ Our site promotes by using Google ad words advertisement, Yahoo Advertising, craigslist personals and casual encounter responses, as well as various singles sites to ensure maximum exposure.

Name: _____ CDC Number: _____

Housing / Cell #: _____

Address: _____ City: _____

State: _____ Zip Code: _____

Song Choice: Please list 1st and 2nd choice in case we are unable to locate your 1st choice

1st Choice _____ 2nd Choice _____

All members of this site will be screened for sex offense registration.

Please Send S.A.S.E along with any request, and or payment, and or photos for returned response.

Incarcerated Bachelors will note bear the burden of postage to return photos.

NO we do not accept postage stamps as payments no exceptions!!

We accept payment by: Institution check, Money Order, and credit card via Pay Pal

LEGAL NOTICE There are no guarantees of responses and no refunds will be provided. If you send more money than is needed, we will not refund the overage; however, you will have credit. Your webpage will be published using the materials that are originally submitted by you and/or any third parties on your behalf—there is a charge for any subsequent changes to your profile except for any mistakes on our part or changes of address. If at the time of initial publication we have received more images or words than your payment allows for and in the absence of instructions from you about which materials to publish, we reserve the right to select which images and/or words to publish and there will be a charge for the publication of the remainder and for any changes to your ad that you desire. It is your responsibility to know the rules and regulations of your facility and to follow them. We will not be held responsible for any damages or harm, disciplinary or otherwise that you incur as a result of placing a pen pal ad with our company. Threats, profanities, or abusiveness of any kind directed towards our staff will result in termination from our site without notice or refund. Supplying false or misleading information is grounds for the immediate and permanent removal of your ad from our website without notice or refund. We will not publish material that is, or that promotes behavior that is, unlawful, harmful, threatening, abusive, sexually explicit, vulgar, obscene, hateful, or racially, ethnically or otherwise objectionable, and we reserve the right to determine what constitutes the foregoing. We reserve the right to refuse service to anyone. We reserve the right at any time, for any reason, to edit, remove, or refuse, in whole or in part, without notice and without refund, any material submitted. Material submitted may be used for our sole benefit in our promotion and advertising.

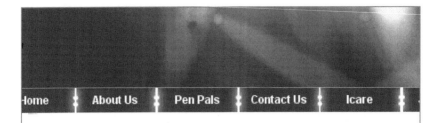

Home | **About Us** | **Pen Pals** | **Contact Us** | **Icare**

Would you like to send an "I Care" support package to an inmate listed on our site?

Welcome to the first ever "I Care" support services pen-pal liaison for those of us who just want to help.

There are currently thousands of inmates who are without the necessary family & friend support that encourages hygiene, nourishment and education assistance.

This pilot program has been designed to aid these registered members of Incarcerated Bachelors Pen-Pals.com that are less fortunate in their ability to support themselves with the basic necessities.

Through "I Care" the voluntary sponsor can email us their intent to utilize this "I Care" support services feature. Please be advised that California inmates are only allowed (1) support package and or special purchase package every quarter.

We in turn will verify if the inmate in question has not received a support package this quarter and you the sponsor will receive a response will receive a response from "I Care" support services within 7-10 business days. The following websites are the approved vending resources for inmates package for your browsing pleasure.

Access Securepakak   Union Supply Direct Walkenhorst PackagesRus

Support a inmate to let them know that you care. The simple act of showing someone you care plants t he seen to positive change.

THE OPRAH WINFREY BLOG

(This is one of several blogs that were posted which were effective in attracting women to Incarcerated Bachelors-PenPals.com)

Eugene L. Weems, Timothy R. Richardson

BLOGS

OPRAH WINFREY WAS RIGHT AGAIN!
By Ms. Jane Doe

Are you tired of looking in all the right places to find the wrong man?

Have you ever thought about looking in all the wrong places for the right man?

True love, friendship and soul mates are found in some of the strangest places, such as through a prison pen pal website

(see www.Incarcerated Bachelors-PenPals.com)

This has brought lonely single women into surprising relationships with an outflowing of passion, affairs of the heart, connections of body, mind and soul, and a sense of oneness with a mate.

Quoted by Oprah Winfrey: *"All the good men are locked up in prison."* Little did I know that she was right on the money, discovery of an untapped treasure of happiness in an unconventional place. Hidden away from society in locked boxes are good men who are handsome, charming, funny, smart, and who can fulfill the full spectrum of a woman's dreams.

So, ladies, if you are willing to step out of your comfort zone, love is only an email away. It worked for me at www.Incarcerated Bachelors-PenPals.com.

Eugene L. Weems, Timothy R. Richardson

THE CRAIGSLIST BAIT

(These are ads that were posted and emailed in
response to ads in the Casual Encounters section)

Eugene L. Weems, Timothy R. Richardson

CRAIGSLIST BAIT POSTINGS

- Long, hard and horny men want to meet women who would like to participate in conjugal visits in a prison environment. Live out your sexual fantasies at www.Incarcerated Bachelors-PenPals.com

- Do you need some thug loving? Fulfill your desires with one of the hot men at www.Incarcerated Bachelors-PenPals.com

- The right men can always be found in the wrong places. Meet handsome, single men of style and swagger at www.Incarcerated Bachelors-PenPals.com

- Do you like hugs, kisses, and that having that love Jones cured? A conjugal visit is what you need at www.Incarcerated Bachelors-PenPals.com

- If you need that cat beaten between your legs with some hard long swipe, pick your punisher at www.Incarcerated Bachelors-PenPals.com

- Handsome men who haven't had sex in years seek women for mind blowing conjugal visits. Choose your lover at www.IncarceratedBachelors-PenPals.com

Eugene L. Weems, Timothy R. Richardson

DAILY CORRESPONDENCE

LOG SHEET

Eugene L. Weems, Timothy R. Richardson

DAILY CORRESPONDENCE LOG SHEET

DATE RECEIVED/POST MARK	NAME	DATE REPLY

Eugene L. Weems, Timothy R. Richardson

BUSINESS CORRESPONDENCE

BIOGRAPHY

Eugene L. Weems, Timothy R. Richardson

BUSINESS CORRESPONDENCE BIOGRAPHY

DATE ACTIVATED: _____
STATUS: _____

PERSONAL

NAME: _____ NICKNAME: _____
AGE: ____ RACE: _____ SEX: _____ SEX.ORI: _____ HT: _____ WT: _____ HAIR: _____ EYES: _____
ADDRESS: _____ E-MAIL: _____
PHONE: _____ WORK: _____
NOTES: _____

INTERESTS/LIKES & DISLIKES

HOBBYS: _____ MUSIC: _____ SONG: _____
COLOR: _____ FOOD: _____ MOVIE: _____ BOOK: _____
VIDEO: _____ SPORTS: _____ RELIGION: _____
CAR/MAKE/MODEL: _____ YR: _____ BOAT/PLANE/RV: _____
PLAY: _____ ACTOR/ACTRESS/ARTIST: _____
ACTIVITIES: _____ CLUB/ORGANIZATIONS: _____
NOTES: _____

FAMILY INFORMATION

MOTHER: _____ AGE: ____ D.O.B: ____ FATHER: _____ AGE: ____ D.O.B: ____
SPOUSE: _____ D.O.B: _____ AGE: ____ OCCUPATION: _____
NOTES: _____

SIBLINGS:
NAME: _____ D.O.B: _____ AGE: ____ OCCUPATION: _____
NAME: _____ D.O.B: _____ AGE: ____ OCCUPATION: _____
NAME: _____ D.O.B: _____ AGE: ____ OCCUPATION: _____
NOTES: _____

CHILDREN:
NAME: _____ D.O.B: _____ AGE: ____ SCHOOL: _____
NAME: _____ D.O.B: _____ AGE: ____ SCHOOL: _____
NAME: _____ D.O.B: _____ AGE: ____ SCHOOL: _____
NOTES: _____

131

Eugene L. Weems, Timothy R. Richardson

SHOOT YO' BEST LINE

www.MYSPACE.com

www.FACEBOOK.com

Eugene L. Weems, Timothy R. Richardson

www.MYSPACE.com

www.FACEBOOK.com

This is another avenue that offers a prisoner unlimited access at opening multiple doors to the hearts of many.

A prisoner could easily have an account open and a webpage designed by a friend or even a company that designs social network pages for a fee. Once the page is designed and Friend Requests have been made, the next step is simply waiting for women to accept your request and respond. The responses will trigger a photo of the woman to be posted as a friend on your webpage.

This is when the *Hook Line* and *Sinker* messages begin.

A *Hook Line* message is used to basically just initiate a response from the target. It's usually a comment that either compliments or questions the target in a fashion that will solicit a response. The *Hook Line* is tailored to the photo of the target. Whatever the response contains is of no real significance, because the real intent is only to open the door for *Sinker* messages to follow.

The *Sinker* message is the most important part of the scheme, which is to get an address or phone number. The *Sinker* message is always basically the same, for example:

Eugene L. Weems, Timothy R. Richardson

HOOK LINES

Eugene L. Weems, Timothy R. Richardson

HOOK LINES

- You look like a movie star! How can I get yo' autograph? Have you read my *About Me* section?
- Wassup? Are you as friendly as you look? Check out my *About Me* section.
- Can I get to know you on a real level? You look like a real down to earth person. Read my *About Me* section. Hope you ain't scared to write a prison, or just too good for it.
- Are you really that cute? Are you too good to holla at a prisoner? Read my *About Me* section. My address is there if you ain't scared.
- Lovin' your smile. The camera loves you. Have you read my *About Me* section? Check it out.
- Wish we could be real friends, 'cause you are so classy! Check out my *About Me* section if you're interested.
- You are very beautiful. Are you as friendly as you are cute?
- Lookin' like a superstar! I bet you're pretty cool peeps, too. I wonder, though, if you're judgmental or down to earth real.
- It's all dat ass your real picture? Wish we could meet for real. Ready my *About Me* section and you might understand (no bail).
- Tell me something good, something new, and something that I don't know, and I'll tell you something different.
- You look like a really fun person to know. Wassup? Check out my *About Me* section.

- You look like my type of lady with style and class. Let's explore this opportunity to get to know each other. Read my *About Me* section for more.

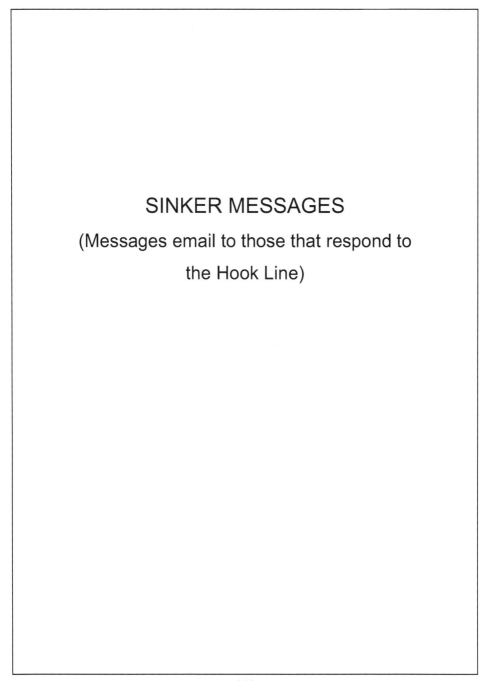

SINKER MESSAGES

(Messages email to those that respond to the Hook Line)

Eugene L. Weems, Timothy R. Richardson

SINKER MESSAGES

Dear Lady,

I appreciate you responding to my message and would love to continue communicating with you on many levels. But my issue is this: I pay for a service through a company that mediates social networking pages for inmates. I have to pay per email message sent and received. So, like I said, I would love to continue communicating with you, as you seem like a really nice, non-judgmental person. There are few in the world who don't scorn the incarcerated. If you would like to snail mail me your address, we could cut out the middle man and save me a few bucks. I promise to have a letter in your mailbox within the week. In it, I will tell you more about me, why I'm here, and what my goals and direction in life has become.

I will try to make you famous with your mailman. Will you let me? If you're afraid or decide I'm not the type of person you could ever be true friends with, I will understand. Take care and create for yourself good days. Hope to able to write, though, if you're open to new things.

Hopefully, your friend,
John Doe

Eugene L. Weems, Timothy R. Richardson

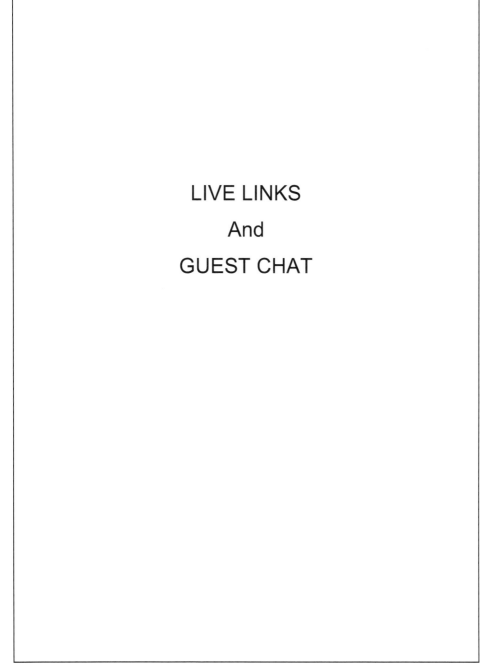

LIVE LINKS

And

GUEST CHAT

Eugene L. Weems, Timothy R. Richardson

LIVE LINKS and GUEST CHAT

There are several telephone chat line companies that offer services for men and women to meet and talk about *no strings attached* arrangements, long-term relationships, or just plain old run your mouth about whatever. But when you're a prisoner and your prison phone calls are time limited to 15 or 30 minutes each, it's sort of like speed chatting when you're trying to get to know someone.

What we would do from within the confines of our little prison bubble would be, first, connect with someone we know personally by calling them collect. (Prison phone calls are always collect) The person we would contact would need three-way calling feature on their home telephone service in order to assist us. Knowing our phone time is limited, we (prisoner) would call and ask our friend who has accepted our collect call to immediately click over and call the Live Links or Quest Chat Line phone number, which we would have at the ready to recite. These chat line phone numbers are easy to obtain, as they are advertised in many magazines and newspapers.

Once our call is connected three-way to the chat line, we (prisoner) would follow the prompts of the recording. Most would require the caller to record a brief description and short message about what you are looking for in a relationship and whether you are available to chat immediately.

We (prisoner) would peruse the recordings left by other callers in search of a suitable target. Once a chat connection has been made, it's time to Shoot yo' best line. In less than ten minutes or so, the prisoner must be charming enough to convince the target to give up their home phone number and/or address for further correspondence.

Eugene L. Weems, Timothy R. Richardson

GRAIN FOR THE BRAIN

Eugene L. Weems, Timothy R. Richardson

GRAIN FOR THE BRAIN

The subconscious is the dominating source of impulsive thought, emotions, desires and abilities. The fact is, you cannot control your subconscious mind, but you can plant the seeds of morals, desires, determination, emotions directed only through habits that influence your subconscious mind.

I am not a psychologist, nor do I aspire to be. What I am is a realist, a person who understands the elements of emotions that cause depression, anger, anxiety and stress. These are the elements of emotions that destroy hopes, dreams, goals and lives. I am confident in saying that we all have experienced all elements of emotions at one time or another in our lives. I know I have many times. My personal experiences taught me how to first become aware of my feelings and potential discomfort that they cause, then to exercise self-discipline when I become angry and not allow negative thoughts to influence my better judgment. The more you deal with it, the more experience you have in countering it. Experience makes you an authority.

I know after reading this book you may have found yourself upset for whatever reason. It's only natural that you would be angry at us (the authors) for having the audacity to compose a book about how we manipulated women for financial gain. Of course you will have mixed feelings about us, along with a few choice unpleasant words. That's quite understandable. Please do vent if you need to; get it out of your system. When you're calmer, you will be able to put things in the right perspective without falling victim to your unchecked emotions that made you angry at first. Please remain mindful that we (the authors) have written this book to help keep women from falling prey to guys like those whom we used to be.

If only you knew, your weakness is just an untapped source of your greatness. Women are the most beautiful creatures on this earth and no man should ever take you for granted.

To the women who have been emotionally hurt by a man; don't dwell on the hardships this has caused, but find what brings you peace of mind and happiness. Realize that everyone is different in their own special way. You are unique. Unique is good. Nobody in the world is exactly like you. Learn to like and love who you are and what you would like to be. Strive to seek positives. You are the only person who can save yourself from drowning in self-depression, hate, distrust and misery. You hold the key to turning on and turning off depression. You can't move on with life unless you move. Today is only here until tomorrow, and believe me, tomorrow will be better.

So keep it real with yourself. Deal with situations you can control. Accept the reality of your own circumstances. And please understand that drugs and alcohol only provide temporary escape from our everyday realities. The problem with temporary escapes is that when your vacation is over, you are forced to return to reality. No matter how low you go, there will be something beneath you. The opposite of hope is hopelessness, so we must deal with the life we are given.

Find your mojo. Nobody is perfect. Find the beauty inside of you. Write a list of all your positives, then focus on one of those qualities each day. The stronger you make your positives, the less your negatives seem to matter. Life is full of ups and downs, but a true champion fights to bring those downs back up again. Find the champion within you.

Some days will be sunny, some days will be raining, but you should still come out and play. Learn to accept the good, the bad and the ugly. If every day was sunny, life would be as dry as the desert. You are remembered for the obstacles you overcome.

Trust me, there is a good, honest man out in the world for you. I now want you to look at yourself in a mirror and say these words twice each and every day: "I am beautiful. I am positive. I am somebody."

Of course you are. You are a queen of Mother Earth.

As I bring my words to an end, I would like to leave you with this reminder of what constitutes a healthy relationship.

A healthy relationship starts by being understanding, considerate, honest, generous, faithful, able and willing to communicate, compromise, sacrifice and work as a team.

It's when two people are willing to put each other's wants and needs first. It's when two people work together to achieve goals to overcome life's trials and tribulations and succeed in living out one another's dreams. It's when you motivate and inspire each other. It's also when your mate offers you a smile that warms your heart, and when they experience some type of pain, it hurts your heart to see it.

It's when your mate's touch takes your breath away. It's about being there through the rough times and enjoying spending quality time together. It's respecting each other's thoughts and opinions. It's forgiving each other's shortcomings and mistakes. It's being able to depend on each other's affection, love, patience, support and understanding. It's when your significant other is the first thought in your mind when you awake and the last before you go to sleep. They'll shower your soul with serenity. It's when you feel complete with a love that is unconditional and unbreakable. It's when your relationship feels as close to perfection as it could get. Last but not least, it's when you can look in the mirror and honestly say, *"I'm sincerely happy."*

The End

Eugene L. Weems, Timothy R. Richardson

To book Timothy R. Richardson for interpersonal Relations consultations and/or speaking engagements please contact:

www.universalpublishingllc.com

GLOSSARY

Eugene L. Weems, Timothy R. Richardson

GLOSSARY

Ballaz: Hood rich, successful drug dealer or financially secure hustler

Bing Bing: A female of Asian/Oriental heritage

Blade: An area known for prostitutes walking and working; a street where they can attract dates in cars to pull over

Boots Laced: Getting information; to get advice or get educated about how to acquire or achieve something

Bucket Bitch: A female who is unattractive and has low self-esteem

Budah Heads: A female of Asian/Oriental heritage

Carpet Broad: Prostitute who considers herself to be a high class escort. She does not stroll the streets looking for dates, but uses casinos, major hotels, and relies on an outcall service to set up her dates

Clients: Customers of prostitutes, escorts, that pay for services rendered

Come up: A task, job or hustle through which money can be made

Double doors and marble floors: Referring to upper class housing in predominantly wealthier areas of suburbia

Game God: The energy of the streets believed to either reward or punish its subjects for their poor decisions and behavior. Members of the street life intent on remaining true to the street life and believe they will be rewarded in forms of profitable gain, good fortune and success

Gigolo: A male who uses his sexual expertise to satisfy women for money, gifts and/or expensive travel

Golden Tongue: Powerful manipulator. A person who has fascinating verbal communication skills used to influence the target

Grain for the brain: Food for thought; information to process; something to think about

Green Bitch: A naïve, trusting female lacking the street smarts to recognize the tactics of urban street life; unfamiliar with particular illegal trades used to earn fast money

Grey Girl: A Caucasian/White female

Hoe: Prostitute

Hoe'cializing: When one prostitute socializes with another prostitute

Incalls: When the prostitute/escort is providing the hosting arrangements for the client/trick to arrive at via appointment to act out their prearranged scenario

Keepin' "em sleep: To avoid educating individuals on the ins and outs of the game; not informing a person what is going on

Knock: When a pimp convinces a female to join his operation

Lot Lizards: Prostitute that uses remote areas as a place to conduct business; such as truck stops, rest stops, all-night business establishments known for abundant traffic, inner city casino parking lots

Mack: A person considered to utilize women for several methods of earnings, such as selling drugs, stealing, check counterfeiting, pick pocketing, and soliciting sex for money

My Groove: A routine or program by which a person remains consistent on a daily basis

Outcalls: Appointments made between prostitutes/escorts and clients/tricks to meet in places arranged and/or owned by the client/trick to rendezvous for the purpose of acting out their agreed scenario

Out of Pocket: When a prostitute/escort breaks the rules

Pimp: A person who will manipulate women into becoming prostitutes for his own profitable game by soliciting strangers to exchange sex for money, which she promptly turns over to her pimp

Pipe Drunk: Intoxicated and stimulated from the pleasures of sexual intercourse and climax

Player: A person who uses his charm and street smarts to develop a method of earnings through manipulation and con games

Pullin' 'em out the air: A person who successfully makes random attempts to meet new women.

Rocked it: Referring to methods by which you execute something, plan, or how you utilized something; how you presented something, accomplished a task remarkably

Rug Rat: Prostitute who considers herself to be an escort that does not walk the streets to solicit sex for sale, but uses casinos, large hotels and outcall arrangements

Scootin' in European: Referring to driving in European luxury cars

Service: When a pimp spends quality time with his hoe; to have sex with her to keep her enthusiastic about her commitment to him

Slanguage: Street vernacular, slang language

Slick Lip: Smooth talker

Snow Bunny: A Caucasian/White female

Soakin' up Game: To learn the rules of the street life hustle and methods of survival of the game

Speil: The verbal language or written wording of one's expressed communication

Square: A person that has for the most part lived a sheltered life; a person that has yet to be exposed to any personal involvements in street hustling within ghetto environments and may even be unaware of the urban slanguage

Square Bear: A person that has for the most part lived a sheltered life; a person that has yet to be exposed to any personal involvements in street hustling within ghetto environments and may even be unaware of the urban slanguage

Stable: A group of prostitutes that are all joined together as one family under the authority of the same pimp

Stayin' in Pocket: When a prostitute abides by all the new rules taught to her by her pimp or fellow prostitutes

Sweatin':   When a pimp is trying to knock or acquaint himself with a prostitute who is ignoring him or trying to evade him

The Game: The economics of street life and the rules that govern it

Tight Eye: A female of Asian/Oriental heritage

Totin' Thumpaz: Carrying firearms

Track: An area known for prostitutes walking and working; a street where they can flag down car dates

Track Star: A prostitute that solicits sex for cash along streets, boulevards, parking lots, pool halls and bars

Turn out: A person considered to be a prospect for manipulation into the transition from Green Bitch or Square Bear to an all out student of The Game when she has completed her very first sexual act in exchange for money

Wakin' the Dead: To avoid educating individuals on the ins and outs of the game; not to inform a person what is going on

Wife-in-Law: Other female prostitutes that work for the same pimp call each other wife-in-law

Eugene L. Weems, Timothy R. Richardson

ABOUT THE AUTHORS

Timothy R. Richardson, aka *TipToe*, is a multi-talented producer and Hip Hop artist and founder of Crime Wave Clothing. He is also co-author of The *Other Side of the Mirror, Head Gamez,* and *Players Exposed.* He is from Oakland, California.

Eugene L. Weems is the bestselling author of *United We Stand* and award winning author of *Prison Secrets.* Weems is co-author of *The Other Side of the Mirror, Head Gamez, and Players Exposed* and *Bound by Loyalty.*

The former kick boxing champion is a producer, model, philanthropist, and founder of No Question Apparel and Inked Out Beef books. He is from Las Vegas, Nevada.

Head Gamez

Eugene L. Weems
Timothy R. Richardson

When a team of four beautiful but deadly assassins are given covert assignments to track down and eliminate Hip Hop's biggest Gangsta Rappers....

"Who gets hit next in this crazy game of killers for hire?"

The world may never find the right man, because sometimes the best man for the job is a woman.

14.95   325 pgs   6x9 Paperback   ISBN: 978-0-9840456-1-7

THE OTHER SIDE OF THE MIRROR

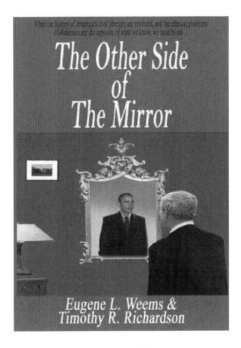

Eugene L. Weems
Timothy R. Richardson

What if Black was White and White was Black?
Could there really be an alternate universe out there?

Join this array of multi-layered characters, each with their own secrets to protect, in their attempts to solve the mystery of the missing President. This story of political intrigue, sexual innuendo and blatant back-stabbing will shock, mystify and intrigue you, with a surprise ending that will leave you breathless!

$14.95   303 pgs   6x9 Paperback   ISBN: 978-0-9840456-0-0

UNITED WE STAND

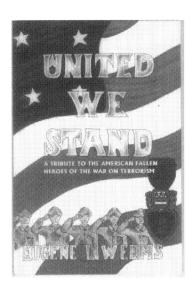

A TRIBUTE TO THE AMERICAN FALLEN HEROES OF THE WAR ON TERRORISM

By Eugene L. Weems

United We Stand is a beautiful collection of inspirational artwork and passion-filled poetry created as a living tribute to the American troops who have made the ultimate sacrifice for our country in the war against terrorism.

100% of the proceeds from this book will be contributed to provide care packages for the active duty troops who remain engaged in the war overseas and provide college scholarship trust funds for the children of our American fallen heroes.

$14.95   95 pgs   6x9 Paperback   ISBN: 978-1-4251-9130-6

Hip Hop/Music

Jackson Ranch Rescue
feline sanctuary

Terri Harper
Founder & President

(916) 362-6068 or 821-1385

11185 Jackson Road
Sacramento, CA 95830

jacksonranchrescue@juno.com

JACKSON RANCH RESCUE Feline Sanctuary is a nonprofit organization which aids abused, abandoned, injured and neglected felines.

We rescue animals in distress whenever an urgent call is received. Our volunteers work with feral cats to help them become familiar with humans so they can be adopted. We have had much success in this area.

Your generous support and assistance is needed. You can help by making a charitable contribution that will go toward the food, shelter and veterinary care, including spay and neuter costs, for these beautiful animals. Your contribution is tax deductible and will be gratefully received.

Contributions can be sent through PayPal using our email address: jacksonranchrescue@juno.com.

THANK YOU FOR YOUR GENEROSITY

15160715R00102

Made in the USA
Lexington, KY
11 May 2012